Surviving PTSD

The Choppy Seas We Deal With

By
The Self-Help Hub

Introduction

A torrent of water rushed over the bow of the ship, submerging the deck in an icy bath. The storm had come suddenly, turning the tranquil sea into a battleground of furious waves and unrelenting wind. Seaman John Everett, with years of experience in the Navy, had seen his share of harsh weather, but this... this was different. His heart pounded in his chest, not only in rhythm with the throbbing of the ship but with a deep-rooted fear that tied itself to an event year past – an event he'd fought so hard to forget. This wasn't just a battle against nature; it was a battle against his past. Against his trauma. Against his Post Traumatic Stress Disorder (PTSD).

John, like an estimated one in eleven people in the United States, was diagnosed with PTSD at some point in their lifetime. This statistic is shocking, yes, but it is not just a number. It represents countless lives disrupted by traumatic events - from veterans like John, survivors of accidents, victims of violence, or anyone who's been thrown into the abyss of terror and emerged forever changed.

Imagine the sea as a metaphor for our minds. Most days, it's calm and manageable. But then, sometimes, a storm hits. It's uncontrollable, overwhelming, and frightening – much like the symptoms of PTSD. The sea doesn't ask for these storms, much like we don't ask for trauma. But, it happens, and when it does, we are left with a choppy sea we need to navigate.

This book, "The Choppy Seas We Deal With: Surviving PTSD", is not just about understanding what PTSD is – it's about you, the sailor, navigating through the choppy waters. It's about facing the storm and learning to survive it. This is not a book filled with complex jargon or unreachable theories; it is a friend who walks alongside you as you embark on this journey. It's a compilation of evidence-based strategies, resources, and practical advice to guide you or your loved ones through the rough seas of PTSD.

In these pages, you are seen, heard, and validated. You are reminded that you are not alone in your struggle. You are empowered to take control of your journey towards recovery. And, most importantly, you are given hope – hope that calm seas are not only possible but are within your reach.

The journey may be rough, but remember, the strongest steel is forged in the hottest fire. This is your journey, your fire, and your opportunity to emerge stronger than ever. The storm doesn't define you; how you sail through it does. So, let's embark on this journey together. Welcome aboard, my friend.

As someone facing PTSD, you are battling not just the internal tempests of fear and anxiety, but also the external ones of societal misunderstanding and stigma. You've probably found yourself floundering in the eye of the storm, desperate for understanding and control over the sudden flashbacks, nightmares, or debilitating anxiety attacks that are trademarks of PTSD. The experience is often accompanied by a feeling of being adrift in a sea of confusion and unpredictability.

One of the primary challenges you might face is learning to manage the symptoms of PTSD. These can range from intrusive memories that replay the traumatic event to physical reactions such as heightened startle responses, insomnia, or difficulty concentrating. Living with these symptoms is akin to being on a ship tossed by wild waves. Just when you think you've gained your footing, another wave of symptoms can knock you off balance, making daily life a struggle.

In addition to the internal challenges, you might grapple with external ones - societal stigma and misunderstanding. Many misconceptions surround PTSD. People may assume it's a sign of weakness, something that only affects veterans, or that individuals with PTSD are unstable or dangerous. Such misconceptions can create a wall of isolation, making you feel unseen, misunderstood, or judged. It's like shouting for help in the middle of a storm, but your voice gets lost in the howling wind.

Navigating relationships while living with PTSD can be like trying to maintain a steady course in choppy waters. The unpredictable nature of your symptoms might cause misunderstandings, tension, or strain in relationships with friends, family, or partners. You may struggle with the fear of being a burden, or feel frustrated when loved ones don't fully comprehend what you're going through.

Seeking help can sometimes feel like reaching for a lifebuoy in open waters, only to grasp at nothing. You might feel lost due to the lack of reliable information, or struggle to find accessible resources or supportive communities. This challenge is made more complicated by the fact that what works for one person may not work for another, making the path to recovery seem even more elusive.

Living with PTSD while trying to maintain your daily responsibilities at work, at home, or in your personal life can feel like you're navigating a ship in a storm while trying to repair its broken parts. You may be battling to keep up appearances, meet deadlines, or care for loved ones, all while dealing with the impact of PTSD.

Navigating through a storm requires a clear understanding of the weather patterns. Similarly, understanding PTSD and its multifaceted nature is the first benefit this book offers. With detailed explanations, the book demystifies PTSD, breaking down its causes, symptoms, and the science behind it in a manner that is easily comprehensible. It is like a chart mapping out the stormy seas, allowing you to comprehend the complexities of your experience.

Beyond understanding, this book also equips you with a toolkit filled with evidence-based strategies and techniques to manage your symptoms. These are practical, hands-on coping mechanisms, like mindfulness exercises, grounding techniques, and lifestyle modifications that can help reduce the severity of PTSD symptoms. Think of these strategies as the tools you would need to fix a leak or maintain balance in your ship during the storm.

The book also serves as a guiding compass for managing your relationships. It offers advice on communication, setting boundaries, and cultivating understanding with your loved ones. This guidance can assist you in navigating the sometimes tumultuous waters of relationships affected by PTSD, fostering stronger connections in the process.

One of the key benefits of this book is its approach towards shedding light on the available resources for managing PTSD. From professional help like therapists and support groups to digital platforms and books, this book introduces a directory of resources to aid your journey. It's like gaining a well-stocked supply of provisions to sustain you during your voyage through choppy seas.

Finally, this book stands as a beacon of hope, a lighthouse on the shoreline guiding you towards the promise of calmer seas. Throughout the chapters, you will encounter stories of resilience and recovery, which serve as a reminder that no matter how intense the storm, it can be survived. It provides the reassurance that peace and recovery are possible, that the storm is temporary, and that clear skies await.

When it comes to PTSD, I understand the journey because I've lived it. I'm not just an author but a survivor of PTSD. This book is more than just a compilation of research and studies; it's a result of my own hard-fought battle against the symptoms and societal misconceptions associated with this disorder.

For years, I grappled with the flashbacks, the anxiety, and the feeling of being constantly on edge. I was in the same storm-tossed boat that many of you may find yourselves in now. I felt the same frustration when people didn't understand what I was going through and the isolation that ensued. I too felt adrift in the sea of uncertainty, longing for some semblance of control over my own mind.

But it wasn't just the storm I experienced. I also experienced the journey towards calm waters. As a student of Psychology, I had the unique opportunity to utilize my professional knowledge to aid my recovery. I spent countless hours diving into scientific research, participating in therapy, exploring various coping strategies, and even making some mistakes along the way.

Throughout my journey, I kept a detailed account of my experiences, the strategies that helped, the resources I utilized, and the relationships I mended. My personal journey as a PTSD survivor has provided me with a unique perspective, one that is both clinically informed and deeply empathetic.

This book is a culmination of that knowledge, experience, and heartfelt understanding. I know what it's like to be in the midst of the storm, but more importantly, I know what it takes to navigate through it. I've witnessed firsthand the transformative power of understanding, coping strategies, support, and resilience in my journey to recovery.

So, I'm not just an author - I'm a fellow sailor who has navigated these choppy waters and reached calmer seas. I believe in the strength and resilience of each person battling with PTSD, and it's my hope that this book will serve as a guide, an anchor, and a source of hope as you navigate your own journey towards recovery.

If you've ever felt lost in the storm of PTSD, struggling to find a lifeline in the midst of crashing waves and unrelenting winds, "The Choppy Seas We Deal With: Surviving PTSD" is the beacon of light you've been searching for. This book is more than a guide - it's your companion, your confidant, and your coach on the journey to reclaim your life from the clutches of trauma. It's time to take back the helm, navigate the storm, and steer towards the calm waters of recovery. Seize this moment, embrace the challenge, and remember - you are not just a survivor, but a warrior.

So, let's begin this journey together, one page at a time. Embark on your journey to recovery - pick up this book and chart your course towards peace and resilience. It's your turn to conquer the choppy seas. Get your copy today!

Chapter 1: Defining PTSD

Post-Traumatic Stress Disorder, known as PTSD, is a term you may have heard quite often. Yet, for many, the true meaning and implication of this condition remain enigmatic. So, let's unravel it together, gently and carefully.

Imagine your brain as a grand library with shelves of books recording your memories, feelings, and experiences. Usually, the librarian - your conscious mind - keeps things in order. But when a traumatic event occurs, it's like a book too distressing to be placed on the shelf. It sits on the librarian's desk, opened and re-read incessantly, causing distress.

PTSD is that unwelcome book which interrupts your life with intense feelings of fear, sadness, or even numbness - echoes of a traumatic past event. These feelings are normal immediately after a traumatic event, but when they persist long afterwards, they may indicate PTSD. It's the brain's reaction to an experience so severe that it disrupts the usual methods of processing and storing memories.

While we often associate PTSD with combat veterans, it's crucial to understand that it can affect anyone who has experienced a traumatic event. This event could range from a severe car accident to experiencing or witnessing violence, enduring natural disasters, or suffering from abuse.

PTSD is complex, unique to every individual. It does not show up in the same way for everyone. Symptoms can include recurring nightmares, feeling on edge, a sense of reliving the trauma, and avoiding anything related to the traumatic event. And these symptoms can interfere significantly with one's day-to-day life.

In this book, we'll explore the facets of PTSD more deeply. We will walk through the winding paths of the brain to understand why PTSD happens, its symptoms, and how it impacts lives. This chapter serves as a steppingstone to your journey towards understanding and managing PTSD, offering a gentle hand of guidance and assurance.

This journey may seem daunting, but remember, you're not alone. We're in this together, navigating the choppy seas, seeking solace and strength. And most importantly, finding ways to place that distressing book back on the shelf.

The Basics of PTSD

Understanding PTSD starts with knowing the fundamentals. The first step in that direction is acknowledging that PTSD is not merely about distressing flashbacks or sudden fits of anger, although these are some of its most recognized symptoms. It's much more complex, affecting individuals in different ways, and at varying intensities.

PTSD is a type of anxiety disorder that develops in response to a traumatic event - an event involving actual or threatened death, serious injury, or a threat to the physical integrity of oneself or others. Experiencing such events can create feelings of intense fear, helplessness, or horror, and these feelings can continue long after the traumatic event has passed.

For individuals with PTSD, their mind continually revisits the traumatic experience as though it is happening again. This occurs through intrusive memories, nightmares, or flashbacks, leading them to avoid reminders of the trauma and to experience negative changes in thinking and mood. This constant reliving can trigger feelings of anxiety, fear, and sadness that can interfere with daily activities and relationships.

Now, let's focus on the key components of PTSD to gain a deeper understanding. These are generally divided into four categories: intrusion, avoidance, negative alterations in cognition and mood, and alterations in arousal and reactivity. Intrusion symptoms refer to the individual experiencing recurring, unwanted, distressing memories of the traumatic event. These could manifest as nightmares or flashbacks, creating a sense of reliving the trauma. Such memories often pop up without warning, disrupting everyday life. They can also be triggered by something that reminds the person of the event, like a certain smell, sound, or sight.

Avoidance, the second component, occurs when individuals go to lengths to avoid thoughts, feelings, or external reminders of the trauma. They may avoid people, places, or activities that could potentially remind them of the traumatic event. This often leads to significant changes in their routines, relationships, or lifestyle. Negative alterations in cognition and mood refer to changes in the individual's thoughts and feelings following the trauma. They may feel detached from others, lose interest in activities they once enjoyed, or persistently experience negative feelings. Some individuals might struggle to remember key aspects of the traumatic event or have distorted thoughts about the event that lead them to blame themselves.

Lastly, alterations in arousal and reactivity are changes in the individual's physical reactions following the traumatic event. These might include being overly alert or on edge, engaging in reckless or self-destructive behavior, having difficulty sleeping, or experiencing angry outbursts.

It's essential to understand that everyone's experience with PTSD is unique. Not everyone will exhibit all these symptoms, and the intensity and combination of symptoms can vary greatly. The manifestation of PTSD depends on several factors, including the individual's personality, the nature of the traumatic event, and their support system.

Another fundamental point is that PTSD does not discriminate. It can affect anyone, regardless of age, gender, culture, or socioeconomic status. While we often hear about PTSD in the context of military combat, many other situations can lead to its development. These might include accidents, natural disasters, serious health problems, or different forms of abuse.

Moreover, it's vital to realize that having PTSD is not a sign of weakness. It's a normal response of the brain trying to deal with abnormal circumstances. Those with PTSD often show incredible resilience in the face of their struggles.

In the next chapters, we'll explore more about the causes of PTSD, its different forms, how it affects individuals and those around them, and effective strategies for managing it. This journey of understanding PTSD can be challenging, but it's a necessary one. Because with understanding comes the ability to foster empathy, provide support, and most importantly, commence the healing process.

By getting familiar with the basics of PTSD, you have taken the first step towards greater understanding and recovery. Remember, this journey is yours to take at your own pace. It's not a race, but a steady voyage towards finding balance amidst the choppy seas. You have the strength to navigate this journey, one step at a time.

Types of PTSD

Just as each person's experience with trauma is unique, so too is their experience with PTSD. The American Psychiatric Association's Diagnostic and Statistical Manual of Mental Disorders (DSM-5) identifies four distinct types of PTSD: Normal Stress Response, Acute Stress Disorder, Uncomplicated PTSD, and Complex PTSD. Let's explore each one of these types in detail.

Normal Stress Response

The Normal Stress Response is a common reaction to a single discrete traumatic event such as a car accident, natural disaster, or incident of sudden violence. People may experience a range of emotional, cognitive, and physical symptoms in the immediate aftermath of such an event. These might include feelings of fear, helplessness, confusion, or even numbness. Physically, individuals may experience a rapid heartbeat, trembling, nausea, or difficulty sleeping. These reactions usually begin to lessen after a few days or weeks. While it may seem strange to include this in a discussion on PTSD, it's important to note that having a normal stress response does not mean you will develop PTSD. However, it does suggest that your mind and body have been affected by the trauma, and it's crucial to monitor your symptoms and seek support if they persist or intensify over time.

Acute Stress Disorder

Acute Stress Disorder (ASD) is a type of PTSD that can occur in the immediate aftermath of a traumatic event, typically within four weeks. Individuals with ASD experience symptoms similar to those of PTSD, including intrusive thoughts, flashbacks, nightmares, and avoidance behaviors.

ASD is a time-limited condition, meaning that for a diagnosis, symptoms must last for a minimum of three days but not more than one month. If the symptoms persist beyond this period, the diagnosis may be updated to PTSD. Early intervention is critical with ASD, as it can help prevent the development of longer-term PTSD.

Uncomplicated PTSD

Uncomplicated PTSD is the most common form of PTSD. It typically follows exposure to a single, discrete traumatic event and is characterized by the presence of the symptoms we have already discussed - intrusion, avoidance, negative changes in mood and cognition, and alterations in arousal and reactivity.

Individuals with Uncomplicated PTSD may find their symptoms interfere with their daily life, causing problems in their relationships, work, or other important areas of functioning. They may have intense, disturbing thoughts and feelings related to their traumatic event, even years after it happened. Despite the challenges, with the right support and resources, recovery from Uncomplicated PTSD is entirely possible. A variety of effective treatments exist, which we will explore in later chapters.

Complex PTSD

Complex PTSD (C-PTSD) arises from exposure to prolonged, repeated, and/or multiple forms of interpersonal trauma, often occurring during critical developmental periods, such as childhood. This type of trauma can include instances of physical or sexual abuse, ongoing emotional abuse, or prolonged periods of neglect.

C-PTSD includes the traditional symptoms of PTSD but also features additional elements such as difficulties with emotional regulation, consciousness, self-perception, and relationships with others. Individuals may struggle with feelings of worthlessness, chronic feelings of emptiness or despair, and may have a distorted perception of their perpetrator, which could include attributing total power to them.

C-PTSD can be a bit more challenging to treat due to its deep-rooted nature and the complexity of symptoms. However, like Uncomplicated PTSD, there are effective treatments available. The key is to seek support from professionals who understand the complexities and are trained in treating trauma.

In conclusion, the journey to understand PTSD is not a straight path, but a winding road that unveils the unique nature of this disorder. By recognizing the different types of PTSD, we become better equipped to understand ourselves or our loved ones, leading to more personalized and effective strategies for managing and overcoming the symptoms. Remember, there's no "right" way to have PTSD. Each person's experience is unique, and that's okay. What's important is to recognize that help is available, and it's okay to reach out. As we progress through this book, we will continue to explore ways to navigate these choppy seas, always remembering that it's the journey, not the destination, that truly counts.

Symptoms of PTSD

Post-Traumatic Stress Disorder, or PTSD, is a complex mental health condition, and its symptoms can be as unique as the individuals who experience them. This makes a "typical" presentation hard to define. However, there are several common symptoms that professionals use as guidelines for diagnosis. They're generally divided into four categories, as defined by the DSM-5:

Intrusion Symptoms

Intrusion symptoms involve reliving the traumatic event. These include:

Recurrent, involuntary, and intrusive distressing memories of the event: These are not mere recollections; they're vivid and distressing, often popping up without warning during the day.

Recurrent distressing dreams or nightmares about the event: Sleep can be disturbed with terrifying dreams replaying aspects of the trauma.

Flashbacks or dissociative reactions: This involves feeling or acting as though the trauma is happening again. For some, these flashbacks can be so intense they lose touch with reality for a time.

Intense psychological distress or physiological reactions to trauma-related cues: Triggers, or reminders of the traumatic event, can bring about strong emotional or physical reactions, like heart palpitations or panic attacks.

Avoidance Symptoms

Avoidance symptoms involve actions taken to evade trauma-related thoughts or external reminders. These symptoms include:

Avoidance of distressing memories, thoughts, or feelings about the event: This might involve avoiding conversations about the trauma or suppressing thoughts about the event.

Avoidance of external reminders of the trauma: This can manifest as staying away from places, people, or objects that remind the individual of the traumatic event.

Negative Changes in Cognition and Mood

This category involves alterations in the individual's thinking patterns and emotional responses following the traumatic event. These include:

Inability to remember an important aspect of the traumatic event: This is not about ordinary forgetfulness but significant chunks of memory loss associated with the trauma.

Persistent and exaggerated negative beliefs or expectations about oneself, others, or the world: The individual may hold beliefs such as "I am bad," "no one can be trusted," or "the world is completely dangerous."

Persistent, distorted cognitions about the cause or consequences of the traumatic event that lead the individual to blame themselves or others: Individuals may feel guilt or shame, believing they were at fault for the traumatic event.

Persistent negative emotional state: This could be constant feelings of fear, anger, guilt, or shame.

Markedly diminished interest or participation in significant activities: The person may stop doing things they once enjoyed.

Feelings of detachment or estrangement from others: They may feel disconnected from loved ones or struggle to maintain close relationships.

Persistent inability to experience positive emotions: They may find it difficult to feel happiness, satisfaction, or love.

Alterations in Arousal and Reactivity

This category includes changes in the individual's arousal and reactivity following the trauma. These symptoms include:

Irritable behavior and angry outbursts with little or no provocation: Individuals may show aggression towards themselves or others.

Reckless or self-destructive behavior: This might involve driving recklessly, substance abuse, or self-harm.

Hypervigilance: They might always be on guard, overly alert to their surroundings.

Exaggerated startle response: They may be easily startled or surprised.

Problems with concentration: They may have difficulty focusing or remembering things.

Sleep disturbance: This might involve trouble falling asleep or staying asleep, or restless, unsatisfying sleep.

These are the primary symptoms of PTSD as categorized by the DSM-5. It's important to note that each individual's experience with PTSD is unique, and not everyone will exhibit all these symptoms. The presence and intensity of these symptoms can also fluctuate over time, sometimes becoming more noticeable during periods of stress or when triggered by reminders of the traumatic event. For a formal PTSD diagnosis, these symptoms should last for more than a month and must cause significant distress or difficulty in social, occupational, or other areas of functioning. It's also crucial to note that these symptoms are not due to medication, substance use, or other illness.

Remember, the recognition of symptoms is not about self-diagnosis but is meant to promote understanding and encourage those affected to seek professional help. If you or someone you know is exhibiting any of these symptoms, it's crucial to reach out to a mental health professional who can provide an accurate diagnosis and guide you toward appropriate treatment.

Understanding the varied and complex symptoms of PTSD allows us to empathize with those suffering from this disorder better. It provides a foundation for the support, treatment, and care required for those navigating the choppy seas of PTSD.

It's okay if you recognize these symptoms within yourself or someone you care about. It can be a daunting realization, but remember, you are not alone. With knowledge comes power - the power to seek help, the power to understand, and ultimately, the power to heal. As we progress further into this book, we will learn more about navigating these choppy waters, always with the aim of reaching calmer seas. The journey might be challenging, but with every wave we cross, we come one step closer to healing and recovery.

What Causes PTSD?

In attempting to understand Post-Traumatic Stress Disorder (PTSD), one question invariably comes up: What causes it?

Let's clarify right away that PTSD is not caused by a personal failing or weakness. It arises from experiencing, witnessing, or learning about a traumatic event that involves actual or threatened death, serious injury, or sexual violation. But why do some people develop PTSD while others, who might have faced similar circumstances, do not? This question points us toward a more nuanced understanding of PTSD's causes.

Traumatic Experiences

The primary trigger for PTSD is exposure to one or multiple traumatic events. These events might include:

Combat and warfare: Veterans and military personnel often face life-threatening situations that can lead to PTSD.

Physical or sexual assault: Survivors of these experiences, whether they occurred in childhood or adulthood, have an increased risk of developing PTSD.

Natural disasters and accidents: Events like earthquakes, floods, fires, or car accidents can lead to PTSD.

Terrorist attacks: Individuals who survive these horrifying experiences can develop PTSD.

Serious health problems or traumatic births: Life-threatening health situations or traumatic childbirth experiences can trigger PTSD.

Witnessing or learning about violence or harm to loved ones: It's not always direct exposure to danger that can lead to PTSD. Sometimes, witnessing harm to others or learning about a loved one's traumatic experience can be enough.

Individual Differences

While traumatic exposure is a requirement for PTSD, not everyone who experiences a traumatic event develops this disorder. Individual differences play a significant role in determining who develops PTSD and who does not. Some factors that might contribute include:

Past mental health issues: Individuals with a history of mental health problems, such as anxiety or depression, are more likely to develop PTSD after a traumatic event.

Family history of mental health problems: Genetics can play a role in PTSD development. If your family has a history of mental health problems, it may increase your risk.

Lack of social support: Individuals with a strong support network are less likely to develop PTSD, while those without such support are at a higher risk.

Repeated trauma: Experiencing multiple traumatic events or ongoing trauma can increase the likelihood of developing PTSD.

Individual coping strategies and resilience: People with robust coping mechanisms and high resilience are less likely to develop PTSD than those with less effective coping strategies.

Personality traits: Certain personality traits, like neuroticism, can increase the risk of developing PTSD.

It's important to emphasize that none of these factors definitively predict who will develop PTSD. They are risk factors, not causes. They increase the likelihood, but it's impossible to predict with certainty who will develop PTSD following trauma.

Biological Factors

Recent research has suggested that biological factors may also contribute to PTSD. Certain changes in the brain and body after a traumatic event might make a person more likely to develop PTSD. Some potential biological factors include:

Changes in the brain's structure or function: Trauma can cause changes in areas of the brain that handle stress and emotion.

Hormonal changes: After a traumatic event, the body's stress response can change, affecting how the body responds to stress in the future.

Genetics: As mentioned above, genetic factors can contribute to the risk of developing PTSD.

Understanding what causes PTSD can help demystify the condition and reduce the stigma associated with it. It can remind us that PTSD is not a sign of weakness or a character flaw but a possible response to traumatic events and experiences. Knowledge of these causes can also guide us towards effective strategies for prevention and treatment, which we will explore in the coming chapters of this book. Remember, understanding is the first step toward healing.

Chapter 2: The Impact of PTSD

Living with Post Traumatic Stress Disorder (PTSD) is akin to navigating the turbulent waves of an unruly sea. The disorder casts a wide and diverse range of impacts on one's life, affecting physical health, mental wellbeing, relationships, and even daily routines. Let's examine these effects in detail to gain a deeper understanding of the challenges faced by those dealing with PTSD.

Physical Health: PTSD isn't solely a mental health issue; it manifests physically as well. From chronic fatigue and headaches to stomach problems and chest pain, the physical toll can be immense. Prolonged periods of stress and anxiety also put an enormous strain on the immune system, making individuals more susceptible to illness.

Mental Wellbeing: PTSD affects mental health beyond the immediate symptoms related to trauma. It often leads to comorbid conditions like depression, anxiety, and substance abuse. Everyday tasks can become mountains to climb, as focus and concentration take a hit.

Relationships: Nurturing relationships while grappling with PTSD can be extremely challenging. There's a risk of emotional isolation, as sufferers might find it difficult to express their feelings or connect with others. Loved ones may feel helpless, not knowing how to provide the right support.

Daily Routines: PTSD can significantly disrupt daily life. Regular routines, such as work, studies, or even simple chores, can become strenuous tasks. Disturbed sleep patterns and nightmares can add to the overall stress, making daily functioning even harder.

Self-Perception: An often-overlooked impact of PTSD is the change in self-perception. Many individuals battling PTSD report feeling detached or distant from their selves, struggling with feelings of worthlessness or guilt. This negative self-perception can hinder the journey to recovery.

It's crucial to remember, though, that everyone's experience with PTSD is unique. The disorder doesn't define you or limit your potential for recovery. Yes, the seas are choppy, but with the right support, understanding, and tools, it's possible to navigate through the storm and find calmer waters.

On the Individual

Your heart pounds like a drum in your chest. You take a shaky breath, struggling to keep your eyes focused. You're not in the middle of a battlefield, but in a grocery store. The overhead lights are too bright; the buzz of conversation is deafening. Each passerby feels like a potential threat. This is a common day in the life of an individual living with Post-Traumatic Stress Disorder.

People with PTSD often experience intense emotional and physical reactions, even when they're not facing any immediate threat. They carry a heightened sense of anxiety, often expecting danger around every corner. This constant state of heightened awareness or 'fight or flight' mode is exhausting and can make even everyday tasks seem insurmountable.

This hyperarousal often results in disturbances in sleep patterns. Falling asleep becomes a Herculean task due to the constant alertness and the dread of nightmares that might ensue. Unfortunately, the lack of restful sleep doesn't provide relief or escape from PTSD's grasp but often exacerbates the symptoms.

Then there's the recurring memories or flashbacks. It's like a movie reel that just won't stop playing. Individuals with PTSD relive their traumatic events, feeling all the fear, pain, and anxiety as intensely as they did during the actual occurrence. It's as if they're stuck in a time loop, forced to replay the worst moments of their life repeatedly.

These flashbacks are often triggered by things that remind them of the trauma. It could be a smell, a sound, a place, or even a person. The triggering event could be seemingly insignificant to others but holds immense power over the person with PTSD, capable of sending them spiraling into anxiety and fear.

Moreover, individuals with PTSD tend to avoid things that remind them of their trauma. This avoidance can become all-encompassing, limiting their lifestyle and making their world smaller. They might steer clear of certain places, people, and activities, even if they once enjoyed them. This avoidance is a protective measure, a desperate attempt to prevent the emotional turmoil associated with these triggers.

Another aspect of PTSD's impact on the individual is the change in beliefs and feelings about oneself and others. Survivors of trauma often grapple with feelings of guilt, shame, or self-blame. They might believe they could have done something to prevent the trauma, leading to self-recrimination and low self-esteem.

Their perception of the world can drastically change, transforming from a place of opportunity to one filled with danger. Trust becomes a casualty in this transformation. It becomes harder to trust others or even themselves, as their own body and mind seem to have betrayed them, subjecting them to continual distress.

Depression and anxiety often coexist with PTSD, adding another layer of complexity to the individual's struggles. The pervasive sadness, loss of interest, and constant worrying can feel like a dark cloud that just won't lift. It's not uncommon for individuals with PTSD to contemplate self-harm or even suicide.

However, it's crucial to remember that although this picture seems bleak, there is hope. Numerous individuals with PTSD have journeyed through this dark tunnel and emerged stronger, taking control of their life once again. Understanding the impact of PTSD on the individual is the first step towards this recovery.

It's also important to emphasize that everyone's experience with PTSD is unique. Each person's symptoms, triggers, and coping strategies can differ. Yet, there's a shared thread of resilience and courage in their stories. Recognizing and appreciating this individuality is key to understanding the condition and building effective strategies for recovery.

The journey towards recovery often involves challenging these altered beliefs, understanding the triggers, and learning effective coping strategies. But the individual doesn't have to walk this path alone. With the support of loved ones and mental health professionals, it is possible to navigate through the stormy seas of PTSD, towards the calm shores of recovery and self-discovery.

On Relationships

You've heard it said that no man is an island. We humans are intrinsically social beings, wired to connect and interact with others. Our relationships form a critical aspect of our lives, influencing our happiness, wellbeing, and even our sense of self. Yet, when Post-Traumatic Stress Disorder comes into the picture, it can cast ripples, even waves, on this social fabric. How does PTSD affect relationships, and what can we do about it? Let's explore.

Living with PTSD often feels like waging a silent, unseen war. Every day brings its own battles, some more challenging than others. Unfortunately, these internal struggles can seep into your relationships, straining connections that once seemed unshakeable.

Communication is the lifeblood of any relationship. It fosters understanding, builds intimacy, and resolves conflict. However, for someone living with PTSD, communication can become a struggle. It's hard to put into words the turmoil you're feeling, let alone explain it to someone else. The fear of not being understood, or worse, being judged, might lead you to close up, creating walls instead of bridges with your loved ones.

Moreover, the symptoms of PTSD—like irritability, hypervigilance, and emotional numbness—can further exacerbate communication challenges. Conversations might quickly escalate into arguments as your tolerance level dips, or you may find yourself withdrawing, unable to engage emotionally. Loved ones may feel like they're walking on eggshells, unsure of what might trigger an episode.

Trust is another essential component of relationships, and PTSD can strain this element too. The world seems unpredictable and dangerous, and your faith in people might have been shattered by your trauma. This broken trust isn't easy to rebuild, and it can create a chasm between you and your loved ones, making it hard for them to reach out and for you to accept their support.

PTSD can also affect your ability to feel positive emotions, a symptom known as emotional numbing. This can make it hard for you to connect with others on a deeper level. Simple pleasures like watching a sunset, sharing a laugh, or enjoying a meal together might lose their joy. This emotional disconnection can leave loved ones feeling helpless and confused, unsure of how to bring back the connection.

For those in a romantic relationship or marriage, PTSD can introduce additional challenges. Intimacy might become a battleground, riddled with anxiety and fear. The partner without PTSD can feel rejected and confused, while the person with PTSD might feel guilty and frustrated. It's like a dance where both partners are listening to different songs, struggling to find their rhythm.

So, how do we navigate these choppy waters? Firstly, by acknowledging the challenges and the impact of PTSD on relationships. It's not easy, and it's not comfortable, but it's a critical step. There's no shame in struggling, and there's immense strength in seeking help. Therapy can be beneficial for both individuals with PTSD and their loved ones. It can provide tools and strategies to manage symptoms, improve communication, and rebuild trust.

Education is another powerful tool. Understanding PTSD, its symptoms, and its impact can replace fear with knowledge, judgement with empathy. The more your loved ones understand what you're going through, the better equipped they'll be to provide meaningful support.

It's also essential to foster self-care and establish boundaries. Both parties need to take care of their mental and emotional wellbeing. PTSD is not an individual's 'problem'; it's a situation that requires collective resilience and compassion.

Remember, healing and reconnecting take time. There will be setbacks along the way, moments of frustration and despair. But there will also be moments of progress, moments when you feel seen, understood, and loved. Hold onto these moments, cherish them. They are beacons of hope, gently guiding you towards a future where PTSD doesn't rule your relationships, but resilience, understanding, and love do. In the next chapter, we'll explore these ideas further, providing practical advice and resources to help you on this journey. Remember, you are not alone. Together, we can navigate these choppy seas.

On Work and Career

In this sea of change that PTSD brings, it's not only the personal life that gets affected, but the professional life also bears its brunt. The workplace is a significant part of our lives, often shaping our identity, providing a sense of purpose, and creating a social environment. However, PTSD can often make it feel like navigating a labyrinth, filled with challenges at every turn.

At work, focus, concentration, and consistency are key, but PTSD can disrupt these cognitive processes. It can feel like trying to complete a jigsaw puzzle while the pieces keep moving or changing shape. Frequent intrusive thoughts or flashbacks can pull your attention away from tasks, leading to decreased productivity and errors. The resulting performance issues can add to the stress, creating a vicious cycle.

Additionally, the symptoms of hyperarousal and heightened alertness can make the work environment seem threatening. The hustle and bustle, the ringing phones, the chatter and laughter, and even the hum of the photocopier can feel overwhelming. You might find yourself constantly on edge, your heart racing at the slightest unexpected noise or movement.

Workplace interactions can also become a source of stress. The social element of work that was once enjoyable can now feel like a minefield. Casual conversations can turn into anxiety-ridden encounters, filled with the fear of potential triggers. The avoidance symptom of PTSD might lead you to withdraw from social situations, limiting your interaction with colleagues and often leading to feelings of isolation.

PTSD can also affect decision-making abilities. The constant second-guessing, the fear of making a mistake, can make even simple decisions feel like a high-stakes gamble. The diminished self-confidence can lead to procrastination, further affecting work performance and productivity.

For those in roles that demand high levels of responsibility or involve frequent encounters with trauma - such as military personnel, firefighters, police officers, or healthcare providers - the impact of PTSD can be even more pronounced. They are often at a higher risk of developing PTSD and may face additional challenges in managing their symptoms within their high-stress work environment.

It's important to note that despite these challenges, having PTSD doesn't mean you are incapable or unfit for work. With understanding, support, and appropriate coping strategies, you can manage your symptoms and continue to contribute meaningfully to your workplace.

One of the first steps towards this goal is understanding your rights as an employee. Many countries have laws in place to protect individuals with mental health conditions from discrimination at work. It might be helpful to consult with a legal expert or mental health advocate to understand these protections and how they apply to you.

Another crucial aspect is communication. Although it might feel daunting, discussing your situation with your employer can open avenues for support and accommodation. This doesn't mean you need to share every detail of your condition. You can choose what you are comfortable sharing and discuss the kind of support or changes that would help you perform your job better.

Examples of workplace accommodations might include a quieter workspace, flexible work hours, the ability to take breaks when needed, and providing written instructions for tasks. Everyone's needs are different, so it's important to consider what changes would be most beneficial for you.

Support can also come in the form of therapy or counseling. Cognitive Behavioral Therapy (CBT) has been found to be particularly effective for managing PTSD symptoms. It can provide strategies for coping with flashbacks, anxiety, and concentration issues, which can greatly improve work performance and overall quality of life.

Lastly, self-care should not be overlooked. This includes taking breaks, managing stress, maintaining a healthy lifestyle, and engaging in activities that you enjoy and that relax you. These practices can help manage your symptoms and improve your emotional resilience, making it easier to handle work-related stresses.

Living with PTSD doesn't mean that your work life is doomed. Yes, there will be challenges, and yes, it might require some adjustments, but you have the strength to rise above them. You have skills, talents, and capabilities that extend far beyond your PTSD. With the right strategies and support, you can navigate through the challenging waves of PTSD in the workplace and continue your journey towards a fulfilling career.

Chapter 3: Common Misconceptions About PTSD

While strides have been made in the general awareness of Post-Traumatic Stress Disorder (PTSD), a number of misconceptions persist. These misconceptions can create barriers to understanding and empathy, hindering the healing journey for many. As we journey through this chapter, we aim to shed light on the common misunderstandings surrounding PTSD.

One of the most widespread misunderstandings about PTSD is that it only affects war veterans. It's true that many veterans do suffer from PTSD; their experiences in war zones can be extremely traumatic. However, PTSD can affect anyone who has experienced or witnessed a traumatic event. This includes survivors of physical or emotional abuse, accidents, natural disasters, or any other serious trauma.

Another misunderstanding is that people with PTSD should be able to simply "get over" their trauma. The reality is, PTSD isn't a condition that a person can will away or overcome with sheer determination. It's a serious mental health condition that requires understanding, patience, and often professional help to manage.

Moreover, there's a myth that if you don't have symptoms immediately after a traumatic event, you don't have PTSD. The truth is, symptoms of PTSD can appear months or even years after the traumatic event occurred.

Through a lens of compassion and understanding, we're starting to see the reality of PTSD. Unraveling these misconceptions is essential not just for people with PTSD, but also for the broader community. By deepening our understanding, we can contribute to a more supportive environment for everyone affected by this condition. This awareness is the first, crucial step towards building a society that not only recognizes PTSD but also fosters acceptance and provides the necessary resources for recovery.

Debunking PTSD Myths

Continuing our journey of understanding, it's vital to confront and debunk the myths about PTSD that, sadly, often circulate. As we explore each myth, we will counter it with the facts, creating a more truthful and compassionate understanding of this challenging condition.

Myth 1: PTSD Only Affects War Veterans

The image of a shell-shocked soldier returning from combat has become synonymous with PTSD. While it's true that many veterans struggle with this condition, PTSD is not exclusive to military service members. Anyone exposed to a traumatic event such as a severe accident, natural disaster, abuse or can develop PTSD. It's essential to recognize this broad impact to ensure that every individual who experiences trauma knows they have the potential for recovery, regardless of their circumstances.

Myth 2: People with PTSD Should "Get Over It"

This myth is particularly damaging because it suggests that recovery from PTSD is simply a matter of willpower. This is not the case. PTSD is a mental health disorder that often requires professional intervention. Individuals with PTSD can't just "get over" their trauma. Healing is a process that takes time, patience, and the right resources. Just as one wouldn't tell a person with a broken leg to "just walk it off," we should not expect those with PTSD to simply shrug off their trauma.

Myth 3: PTSD Symptoms Appear Immediately After the Trauma

It's often thought that PTSD symptoms appear right after a traumatic event. This is not necessarily true. PTSD symptoms can manifest months or even years later. This delay can lead to confusion and the false assumption that something else might be causing the distress. Recognizing this fact can help both individuals and healthcare providers identify PTSD and begin treatment even if significant time has passed since the trauma.

Myth 4: People with PTSD are Violent or Dangerous

Often influenced by media portrayals, some believe that individuals with PTSD are volatile or unpredictable. The truth, however, is quite different. Most individuals with PTSD are not violent. Instead, they are much more likely to withdraw from others or be on guard, as they might be wrestling with anxiety, depression, or the need to avoid reminders of their trauma.

Myth 5: PTSD is a Sign of Weakness

This misconception might be one of the most harmful. It suggests that only those who are mentally weak develop PTSD after a traumatic event. However, PTSD has nothing to do with mental fortitude. The reality is that trauma can affect anyone, regardless of their mental strength.

By insisting that PTSD is a sign of weakness, we discourage people from seeking the help they need. It's essential to understand that seeking assistance is not a sign of weakness but a courageous step toward healing.

Understanding these myths and countering them with the truth helps to alleviate some of the stigmas associated with PTSD. The process of debunking these myths invites compassion, empathy, and understanding. It underscores the fact that PTSD is not a sign of weakness, nor is it a condition that someone can merely "get over".

Instead, PTSD is a response to trauma that can affect anyone. It's not always immediate, it's not limited to veterans, and it does not predispose people to violence. It's a complex disorder that requires patience, understanding, and professional care.

Through understanding, we can contribute to a more supportive and knowledgeable environment for individuals living with PTSD. By replacing myths with facts, we can create a better path to recovery, one that leads to acceptance, not judgment, and to support, not stigma. As we navigate this path together, we can find hope and foster resilience, creating a more enlightened perspective on PTSD, which is integral to the journey of recovery.

Understanding the Stigma

As we continue our exploration into the world of PTSD, we arrive at a significant barrier that many individuals face: stigma. Understanding the stigma associated with PTSD is a crucial part of fostering empathy, offering support, and ultimately aiding the process of recovery.

Stigma is a societal mark of shame or discredit, and it can often lead to discrimination. When it comes to mental health, and PTSD in particular, stigma can have far-reaching implications. It might be subtle, such as a friend withdrawing their companionship, or more direct, such as workplace discrimination. No matter the form it takes, stigma creates an additional layer of challenge for individuals living with PTSD.

So why does stigma exist? Many factors contribute to it. One primary contributor is the general lack of understanding about PTSD. As we've already discussed, myths and misconceptions about PTSD are rampant. They perpetuate harmful stereotypes and foster an environment where individuals with PTSD are misunderstood or judged harshly.

For instance, the myth that people with PTSD are violent or dangerous can lead to fear and avoidance. Similarly, the misconception that PTSD is a sign of mental weakness may make others view those with PTSD as flawed or less capable. These falsehoods create a negative and inaccurate picture of PTSD, and, by extension, those living with it.

Media representation also plays a role in reinforcing stigma. Often, PTSD is portrayed dramatically or inaccurately in movies, television shows, and other media, leading to misconceptions about the condition. For example, the notion that everyone with PTSD has severe, uncontrollable reactions to triggers is a common trope in media but is not universally true. This oversimplification reduces the complexity of PTSD to sensationalized moments, further perpetuating misunderstanding and stigma.

Moreover, societal attitudes towards mental health as a whole can contribute to the stigma surrounding PTSD. Some cultures or societies might view any mental health issues as a sign of weakness or personal failing. This perspective can discourage people from seeking help, fearing judgment or ostracism.

Stigma not only impacts how society views people with PTSD but also how those individuals view themselves. This internalized stigma can lead to feelings of shame, guilt, and worthlessness. It can discourage people from seeking help, creating a significant barrier to recovery.

However, it's important to note that stigma, like the myths we've discussed, is based on misconceptions, not reality. The truth is that having PTSD is not a personal failing or a sign of weakness. It's a human response to trauma, and it's something that requires understanding and support, not judgment or fear.

To combat this stigma, education is vital. The more people understand about PTSD, the more they can empathize with those living with it. And the more empathy we have, the more the walls of stigma begin to crumble.

As we become more knowledgeable about PTSD, we can challenge stereotypes, correct misconceptions, and contribute to a more compassionate society. Understanding the truth about PTSD and sharing that understanding with others can help create a world where people with PTSD are seen for who they truly are, not as their condition.

In this world, those affected by PTSD can feel more comfortable seeking the help they need. They can feel less isolated, less misunderstood, and more hopeful about their ability to recover. This is the world we should strive to create—a world where stigma gives way to understanding, where judgment gives way to compassion, and where shame gives way to resilience.

This understanding won't eliminate the challenges of living with PTSD, but it can make the path to recovery less daunting. As we move forward, let's take these truths with us: PTSD is not a sign of weakness, people with PTSD are not inherently dangerous, and everyone deserves understanding, support, and respect in their journey to recovery. This path isn't easy, but by walking it together, we can help alleviate the burden of stigma, and in doing so, move one step closer to a more accepting and empathetic world.

The Reality of PTSD

Having debunked the myths and shed light on the stigma surrounding PTSD, let's now turn our attention to the real-life experiences of those living with this condition. Understanding the reality of PTSD is key to providing the support, empathy, and resources needed for recovery.

PTSD is not just a single experience, nor is it a one-size-fits-all condition. It's a complex mental health disorder with a range of symptoms that can vary greatly from person to person. Some may experience intrusive memories and flashbacks, while others might deal with emotional numbness, and yet others might struggle with hyperarousal, such as being easily startled or feeling always on edge.

People living with PTSD might have good days and bad days. There may be periods of relative calm, followed by times of intense distress. These fluctuations can often make it challenging to predict or understand one's own reactions, adding another layer of complexity to the experience of PTSD.

Moreover, PTSD doesn't just affect the person diagnosed with the condition — it also has an impact on their loved ones. Family members and friends might feel at a loss on how to provide support, or they may struggle to understand the changes they see in their loved one.

The reality of PTSD is also shaped by each individual's unique experience of trauma. What might be a manageable situation for one person can be deeply traumatic for another, and it's crucial to respect these differences. It's not about comparing traumas or judging who had it worse; it's about acknowledging each person's individual experience and offering empathy and understanding.

Dealing with PTSD can often feel isolating. The person may feel misunderstood or disconnected from those around them. This isolation can make the journey to recovery more challenging, emphasizing the importance of supportive relationships and understanding communities.

One significant part of the reality of PTSD is the possibility for recovery. While PTSD can be a long-term condition, it's crucial to remember that with the right support and treatment, individuals can learn to manage their symptoms and lead fulfilling lives. Recovery doesn't necessarily mean a complete absence of symptoms, but rather finding ways to cope, regaining control, and creating a new normal.

Understanding the reality of PTSD means recognizing the strength and resilience of those living with this condition. It means acknowledging their struggles without judgment and offering support and understanding. It means seeing them as individuals, not just as their diagnosis.

Indeed, PTSD is a challenging condition, but it does not define a person. People with PTSD are more than their trauma — they are parents, children, friends, colleagues, and much more. They have hopes, dreams, abilities, and potential. They deserve to be seen, understood, and respected.

In the end, the reality of PTSD is a human story. It's a story of experiencing trauma and dealing with its aftermath. It's a story of struggle and resilience, of pain and healing, of fear and courage. It's a story that deserves to be heard, understood, and met with empathy and compassion. As we continue on this journey together, let's carry this understanding with us. Let's use it to guide how we interact with those living with PTSD, and let's use it to create a world where people with PTSD are seen, heard, and supported. This isn't just about understanding PTSD — it's about understanding people, fostering empathy, and ultimately, creating a world where everyone feels seen and supported in their journey to recovery.

Chapter 4: Understanding Trauma

Every life is touched by events that shake us, disrupt our routine, and leave us changed. These are defining moments, turning points, if you will, where the world as we know it is never the same again. When such events are intensely distressing or threatening, they bear the name of trauma.

In our journey towards healing from Post-Traumatic Stress Disorder (PTSD), it's crucial to understand what trauma is and how it impacts our lives. Our aim in this chapter is to unravel the complex nature of trauma in a compassionate and understandable manner.

First and foremost, trauma is not an event itself but our emotional response to it. It's a deeply distressing or disturbing experience that overwhelms our capacity to cope, causing feelings of helplessness, reducing our sense of self, and our ability to feel a full range of emotions. Traumas come in many shapes and sizes. Some, like natural disasters, accidents, or violence, are sudden and clearly identifiable. Others, like prolonged emotional abuse, may be less visible but equally damaging.

Our reactions to trauma are as diverse as we are. Each person is unique in how they process and respond to traumatic experiences. Some might feel an immediate shock, while others might not recognize the impact until much later when certain symptoms start to surface. This is often the case with PTSD, which might not become evident until long after the initial trauma.

Understanding trauma is a crucial step in our journey towards healing. When we can identify and acknowledge what happened to us, we are better equipped to begin the process of recovery. By recognizing the profound impact of trauma, we can begin to make sense of our feelings and behaviors and start to regain control over our lives.

This chapter seeks to guide you gently through the maze that is trauma. It is designed to give you a clearer perspective of what you're dealing with and offer insight into how trauma changes us. Ultimately, by gaining knowledge and insight, we can empower ourselves to begin the journey towards recovery.

How Trauma Affects the Brain

When we face a traumatic event, it is not just our minds that are impacted; our brains also bear the brunt. The effects of trauma on the brain are significant and help explain many of the challenges encountered by those dealing with PTSD. In this section, we will take a comprehensive look at how trauma interacts with our brain and influences our behavior and thought processes. At the heart of our response to trauma is a part of the brain called the amygdala. This almond-shaped bundle of neurons plays a crucial role in processing emotions, especially fear. When a traumatic event occurs, the amygdala goes into overdrive, signaling that we are in danger. This triggers what we often refer to as the 'fight, flight, or freeze' response. Adrenaline floods our system, our heart rate increases, and we become hyper-alert to potential threats.

This response is natural and necessary. It's our brain's way of protecting us, preparing us to either confront the danger or escape it. However, in the case of PTSD, this response system can become stuck. The brain continues to perceive danger even when it no longer exists. This explains why individuals with PTSD can have intense reactions to triggers that remind them of the trauma - the brain is responding as if the traumatic event is happening all over again.

Meanwhile, the prefrontal cortex, the area of the brain responsible for reasoning and decision-making, can become less active after a trauma. This part of our brain helps us make sense of our experiences, think logically, and control impulsive reactions. When it's not working as effectively, it can make it harder for individuals with PTSD to control their emotions, leading to feelings of being overwhelmed or out of control.

The hippocampus, another vital brain region affected by trauma, is responsible for creating and organizing memories. High levels of stress hormones released during trauma can interfere with its functioning, leading to difficulties in memory. This might be why some people find their memories of the trauma are disorganized or fragmented. They may struggle to remember certain details or feel as if they're reliving the trauma when they recall it.

Additionally, the constant state of high alert and stress experienced by those with PTSD can have a wear-and-tear effect on the brain and the body. Chronic stress can affect the brain's structure and function, impact our immune system, and increase the risk of various physical health problems.

In understanding how trauma affects the brain, we can better comprehend the many symptoms of PTSD. It's not just about being unable to 'move on' or 'let go' of the traumatic event. The changes that occur in the brain can make it genuinely challenging to manage emotions, control reactions, and process memories.

However, it's crucial to keep in mind that our brains are not fixed in stone; they are incredibly adaptable. This trait, known as neuroplasticity, means that our brains can change and adapt throughout our lives. With the right support and treatment, it's possible to 'retrain' the brain, helping it to react less intensely to triggers and manage stress more effectively. This is the underpinning philosophy of many treatments for PTSD, and we will discuss this further as we explore coping strategies and therapies.

Understanding the relationship between trauma and the brain can help reduce some of the shame or guilt you might feel about your symptoms. It's not a sign of weakness or a character flaw; it's a physiological response to an overwhelming event. By recognizing this, we can treat ourselves with more kindness and patience, creating a more supportive environment for recovery.

Types of Traumas

Trauma is not a one-size-fits-all experience. It comes in various forms, affects individuals differently, and thus, requires distinct approaches for treatment. Let's examine different types of traumas, their specific symptoms, and potential treatments.

1. Acute Trauma

Acute trauma results from a single distressing event. This might be a violent attack, a natural disaster, a severe accident, or a sudden loss. The event is often life-threatening or perceived as such, leaving a person feeling extreme fear, a sense of helplessness, or horror.

Symptoms of acute trauma can vary widely, from flashbacks and nightmares about the event to physical symptoms like headaches or nausea. People may experience difficulty sleeping, increased irritability, or have a constant feeling of being on edge.

Treatment often involves trauma-focused cognitive-behavioral therapy (TF-CBT), a type of therapy that helps individuals process their traumatic experiences in a supportive environment. Eye movement desensitization and reprocessing (EMDR) can also be useful, a method that uses eye movements guided by a therapist to help people process and make sense of their traumatic memories.

2. Chronic Trauma

Chronic trauma is the result of prolonged exposure to highly stressful situations. Examples can include ongoing physical or emotional abuse, living in a war-torn region, or enduring long-term severe illness.

Symptoms may be similar to those of acute trauma but are often more complex due to the long-term nature of the exposure. These can include severe anxiety, depression, difficulties in forming healthy relationships, feelings of detachment or disassociation, and destructive behaviors such as substance misuse.

Treatment can be a longer-term process and may involve a combination of therapies. This could include TF-CBT or EMDR, along with exposure therapy, where the individual is gradually and safely exposed to the thoughts, feelings, and situations that remind them of the trauma.

3. Complex Trauma

Complex trauma describes multiple traumatic events, often invasive and interpersonal, occurring within specific timeframes and specific relationships. These events often take place early in life and can disrupt many aspects of the child's development and the formation of a sense of self.

People who have experienced complex trauma often have difficulties regulating their emotions, struggle with their self-perception, have a distorted perception of the perpetrator, and experience difficulties in relationships.

Therapy for complex trauma typically involves a multistage approach. Initially, the focus is on establishing safety and stability in the person's life. Following that, the individual and therapist work together to process the trauma. Ultimately, the focus shifts to helping the person integrate their experiences and move towards recovery.

4. Secondary Trauma

Also known as vicarious trauma, this form occurs when an individual is exposed indirectly to a traumatic event through the first-hand account or narrative of that event by another. Common in caregivers or loved ones of people who have experienced trauma, or professionals such as therapists, police, and journalists, secondary trauma can have serious effects.

Symptoms often mirror those of direct trauma, such as intrusive thoughts, chronic fatigue, sadness, anger, poor concentration, and detachment.

Care strategies for secondary trauma involve self-care techniques to manage stress and avoid burnout. This could include regular exercise, good nutrition, ample sleep, and leisure activities. In addition, therapy and support groups can provide a space for sharing experiences and learning coping strategies.

5. Historical Trauma

Historical trauma refers to trauma experienced by specific cultural, racial, or ethnic groups due to historical oppression or events. The trauma is not individual but shared among the group, and its effects can be passed down through generations, causing a ripple effect of trauma responses.

Symptoms can manifest as psychological issues, substance misuse, poor physical health, and chronic disease. The feelings of trauma can be triggered by events that remind individuals or communities of past traumas.

Healing and treatment strategies involve culturally sensitive and community-specific approaches. This could include community healing efforts, traditional healing practices, storytelling, and education.

As we understand that trauma comes in various forms, it allows us to better understand its effects on individuals. Each person's response to trauma is different, and thus their path to recovery will be too. As we explore the diverse types of trauma, their specific symptoms, and potential treatments, we are better equipped to extend empathy to ourselves and others affected by trauma. This knowledge is also crucial for healthcare professionals to provide the most suitable care for those affected by different types of traumas.

Chapter 5: PTSD and Comorbidities

As we further our understanding of PTSD, it's important to acknowledge that for many individuals, this condition doesn't exist in isolation. Instead, PTSD can often coexist with other mental health conditions, a concept known as comorbidity. In this chapter, we'll explore the complex relationship between PTSD and comorbid conditions, shedding light on why they often occur together and how this impacts the treatment and recovery process.

A comorbid condition is a separate but related disorder that occurs in conjunction with another. For instance, a person diagnosed with PTSD might also experience depression, anxiety, or substance use disorders, among others. These comorbid conditions can exacerbate the symptoms of PTSD, complicate its treatment, and add to the challenges that individuals face.

Why does this happen? The reasons are complex and multifaceted, encompassing biological, psychological, and environmental factors. Trauma impacts the brain in profound ways, potentially making an individual more susceptible to other mental health conditions. At the same time, the psychological distress and lifestyle changes associated with PTSD can also contribute to the development of these comorbid conditions.

Understanding comorbidity is crucial to effectively supporting individuals with PTSD. A comprehensive treatment approach that addresses not only the PTSD but also the comorbid conditions can be instrumental in aiding recovery. It also underscores the importance of comprehensive mental health care, in which various aspects of an individual's mental health are considered and addressed. The journey through PTSD is unique for each person, and the presence of comorbid conditions can add further individual variation to this journey. Recognizing this complexity can help us to better empathize with, support, and aid those living with PTSD in their path towards recovery. In the coming discussions, we will delve deeper into some of the most common comorbid conditions associated with PTSD, in hopes of broadening our understanding and enhancing our ability to support those affected.

Depression and PTSD

The intertwined relationship between Post Traumatic Stress Disorder (PTSD) and depression forms a crucial part of the discourse on mental health. While they are distinct disorders, the high prevalence of comorbidity necessitates a comprehensive understanding of their interplay and its implications for individuals navigating their paths towards healing.

Depression is a debilitating condition characterized by persistent feelings of sadness, loss of interest or pleasure in activities, changes in appetite and sleep patterns, feelings of worthlessness, and in severe cases, thoughts of death or suicide. It has a profound impact on an individual's life, affecting their thoughts, feelings, and ability to carry out daily tasks.

PTSD, on the other hand, is a mental health disorder that arises in response to experiencing or witnessing a traumatic event. Its symptoms include recurrent distressing memories or flashbacks of the trauma, avoidance of reminders of the event, negative changes in thoughts or mood, and alterations in arousal and reactivity.

When these two conditions coexist, they create a complex web of emotional, cognitive, and physiological symptoms that can complicate the treatment process and intensify the overall distress experienced by the individual. Let's explore how this intersection can manifest and its potential impact.

Depression and PTSD can influence each other in multiple ways. The chronic state of hyperarousal and the recurrent traumatic memories associated with PTSD can lead to exhaustion and despair, laying the groundwork for depression. Similarly, the negative changes in thoughts and mood, such as feelings of guilt or worthlessness and difficulty feeling positive emotions, can both be part of PTSD and depressive symptomatology.

The co-occurrence of depression and PTSD can make it harder for individuals to function in their daily lives. The constant re-experiencing of traumatic memories characteristic of PTSD can be debilitating, and when coupled with the energy-draining effects of depression, it can lead to significant impairment in social, occupational, and other important areas of functioning.

People suffering from both PTSD and depression may also exhibit a higher degree of avoidance behavior. This could mean avoiding people, places, or things that remind them of their trauma, but also activities they once enjoyed or tasks they need to accomplish. The world can become overwhelming, further contributing to social isolation and feelings of hopelessness.

Moreover, those with coexisting PTSD and depression face a higher risk of developing additional mental health issues, such as anxiety disorders and substance use disorders. They may also be more likely to experience suicidal ideation or engage in self-harming behaviors, making their situation not just a mental health concern, but also a matter of immediate safety.

Despite these challenges, it's important to hold on to the fact that recovery is indeed possible. The key lies in comprehensive treatment approaches that address both conditions simultaneously. Treatment plans usually involve psychotherapy, medication, or a combination of both. Cognitive Behavioral Therapy (CBT), in particular, has shown to be effective in treating both depression and PTSD.

CBT for depression often involves learning to identify and challenge negative thought patterns and develop healthier coping strategies. For PTSD, trauma-focused CBT can help individuals process their trauma and manage their symptoms. It's crucial that any therapeutic intervention provides a safe space for the individual to explore their experiences and feelings.

Moreover, the role of social support and self-care cannot be underestimated. Connection with others can serve as a powerful counterforce to the isolation and hopelessness that both PTSD and depression can instigate. Physical activity, adequate sleep, nutrition, and relaxation exercises can also play a part in managing symptoms and promoting overall wellbeing.

This discussion underscores the complexity of mental health and the intricacies involved when dealing with coexisting conditions like depression and PTSD. However, with knowledge and understanding, we are better equipped to navigate these complexities, and most importantly, to extend our empathy, support, and resources to those wrestling with these intertwined conditions. The journey might be challenging, but with the right tools and support, it is a journey that can certainly lead to recovery and rediscovery of one's strengths and capabilities.

Anxiety Disorders and PTSD

The relationship between Post Traumatic Stress Disorder (PTSD) and anxiety disorders forms a critical part of understanding the many facets of PTSD. An individual grappling with PTSD may also be confronted with an anxiety disorder, adding another layer of complexity to their experience. Thus, shedding light on the connection between these disorders becomes crucial in providing comprehensive support and effective treatment strategies.

Firstly, it's important to understand that while PTSD itself is categorized under the umbrella of 'trauma and stressor-related disorders,' it shares numerous symptoms with 'anxiety disorders.' These shared symptoms can include hypervigilance, excessive worry, and intrusive thoughts, which might often lead to confusion or misdiagnosis. Anxiety disorders encompass a wide range of specific conditions, each with its own set of characteristics. These include Generalized Anxiety Disorder (GAD), characterized by excessive worry about everyday matters; Panic Disorder, where an individual experiences repeated panic attacks; Social Anxiety Disorder, marked by a profound fear of social or performance situations; and various Phobic Disorders, involving intense fear of specific objects or situations.

The manifestation of an anxiety disorder alongside PTSD can compound the distress experienced by the individual. For instance, an individual with PTSD may also suffer from GAD, with constant worry and fear amplifying the traumatic stress symptoms. Or someone might experience Panic Disorder along with PTSD, where panic attacks may be triggered by reminders of the traumatic event.

The interplay of these disorders can intensify feelings of fear, making the world seem perpetually dangerous. It can lead to avoidance behaviors, where individuals steer clear of situations or environments, they fear might trigger a panic attack or a traumatic memory. This avoidance can further narrow their world, leading to isolation and a reduced quality of life.

People living with PTSD and concurrent anxiety disorders might also face difficulties in concentrating, sleeping, or carrying out everyday tasks. They might be persistently on edge, anticipating danger at every turn. This constant state of arousal can be physically and emotionally draining, leading to exhaustion and despair.

However, the presence of an anxiety disorder alongside PTSD does not signify an insurmountable obstacle to recovery. Rather, it underscores the need for a holistic treatment approach that addresses both conditions. Therapy, such as Cognitive Behavioral Therapy (CBT), can be incredibly effective in this regard.

CBT techniques can be tailored to the specific anxiety disorder. For instance, exposure therapy can be beneficial for phobias, while cognitive restructuring can help individuals with GAD challenge and change their worry thoughts. When combined with trauma-focused CBT for PTSD, individuals can learn to manage their anxiety and control their PTSD symptoms effectively.

Similarly, certain types of medication can also be effective in treating both PTSD and anxiety disorders. Selective serotonin reuptake inhibitors (SSRIs) and serotonin and norepinephrine reuptake inhibitors (SNRIs), for instance, can help alleviate symptoms of both conditions.

It's also crucial to emphasize the importance of self-care in managing these conditions. Regular exercise, a healthy diet, adequate sleep, and mindfulness techniques can help reduce anxiety and enhance overall well-being. Moreover, social support plays a pivotal role in recovery. The understanding and empathy from loved ones can serve as a vital source of strength and encouragement.

In the end, understanding the relationship between PTSD and anxiety disorders empowers us to better support those living with these conditions. With the right knowledge and resources, individuals can navigate their path towards healing and regain a sense of control over their lives. The journey may be challenging, and the road may be long, but with patience, resilience, and the right support, progress is not just possible, it's probable. The ultimate goal is to ensure that individuals are not defined by their conditions, but rather acknowledged for their strength and resilience in their journey towards recovery.

Substance Abuse and PTSD

Post Traumatic Stress Disorder (PTSD) is an intricate condition with implications that can extend far beyond the realm of trauma alone. One of the most common and concerning co-occurring issues faced by individuals with PTSD is substance abuse. This intertwining of conditions can further complicate the journey towards healing, making it vital to understand and address this dual diagnosis effectively.

When we talk about substance abuse in the context of PTSD, it generally refers to the misuse of alcohol or drugs, whether they be prescription medications or illicit substances. A person might turn to these substances as a coping mechanism, seeking temporary relief from the overwhelming symptoms of PTSD. However, this form of self-medication often brings about more harm than relief in the long run.

The reasons behind substance use can vary greatly among individuals with PTSD. For some, it could be an attempt to numb the distressing memories of a traumatic event. For others, substances might offer a way to combat sleep disturbances or feelings of hyperarousal. Yet for all, this path holds the potential for addiction, creating a cycle that further complicates their mental health landscape.

Indeed, the relationship between PTSD and substance abuse is a two-way street. Just as PTSD can lead to substance misuse, so too can substance misuse exacerbate PTSD symptoms. For example, while alcohol or drugs may momentarily ease PTSD-related anxiety, their effects wear off after a short period, often causing anxiety levels to spike even higher than before. This escalating cycle can intensify PTSD symptoms and make them more challenging to manage.

Furthermore, substance abuse can hinder the effectiveness of PTSD treatment. If a person is regularly consuming alcohol or drugs, they may find it more difficult to engage fully in therapy, remember coping strategies, or maintain the motivation needed to work towards recovery.

Acknowledging the intersection between PTSD and substance abuse is crucial for effective treatment. This calls for an integrated approach that addresses both conditions simultaneously. Failure to treat both conditions can lead to a vicious cycle where untreated PTSD symptoms encourage substance use, which in turn makes the PTSD symptoms worse.

The good news is that there are effective treatment strategies available for individuals facing this dual diagnosis. Cognitive Behavioral Therapy (CBT), for instance, has been proven effective in treating both PTSD and substance abuse. CBT can help individuals understand the link between their thoughts, feelings, and behaviors, and equip them with skills to manage their symptoms and reduce substance use.

Medication can also be an important component of treatment. Certain medications can be effective in reducing cravings, managing withdrawal symptoms, and treating PTSD symptoms. However, it's crucial that this is overseen by a healthcare professional who can monitor the individual's progress and make adjustments as necessary.

Beyond therapy and medication, social support plays an instrumental role in recovery. Having a network of supportive individuals can provide a sense of belonging and understanding, reducing feelings of isolation and hopelessness. Moreover, support groups can be an invaluable resource, offering a safe space to share experiences, gain insight from others who have walked a similar path, and find encouragement in the collective journey towards recovery.

PTSD and Physical Health

When thinking of Post-Traumatic Stress Disorder (PTSD), our thoughts often gravitate toward the mental and emotional anguish it carries. It's important, however, to remember that PTSD doesn't exist in isolation - it can have substantial effects on physical health as well. This reality makes it crucial for anyone dealing with PTSD, or those supporting someone who is, to understand its potential physical health implications.

So, how exactly does PTSD impact physical health? In many ways, the psychological distress triggered by PTSD can set off a domino effect that reaches various areas of physical wellbeing. The body and mind are interconnected, and when one suffers, the other can too.

Sleep disturbances, for instance, are a common symptom of PTSD. Trauma can result in nightmares or insomnia, leading to a lack of restorative sleep. This deprivation can impact various aspects of physical health, including the immune system's functioning, energy levels, and cognitive processes. Over time, chronic sleep deprivation can even increase the risk of developing conditions like heart disease and diabetes.

Stress is another pervasive issue for individuals dealing with PTSD. The body's stress response is essentially a survival mechanism, designed to protect us from immediate danger. However, for those living with PTSD, this response can be frequently activated, leaving them in a state of chronic stress. Over time, this can put excessive strain on the body, leading to high blood pressure, heart disease, and other stress-related illnesses.

Physical symptoms like headaches, dizziness, chest pain, stomach problems, and musculoskeletal pain can also arise in the wake of PTSD. The mind-body connection is strong, and the distress associated with PTSD can manifest as physical symptoms. It's important to not dismiss these symptoms as "all in the mind", but to recognize them as genuine physical experiences connected to psychological distress.

It's also worth noting that individuals with PTSD are at a higher risk of engaging in behaviors that can harm physical health. This could include substance abuse, as we discussed earlier, but also extends to other harmful behaviors such as poor diet, lack of exercise, and even self-harm.

Given these potential implications, it's crucial to take an integrated approach to care that not only addresses the psychological components of PTSD but also promotes physical wellbeing. This may include a balanced diet, regular exercise, and adequate sleep. Mind-body therapies like yoga and mindfulness meditation can also be beneficial, helping to cultivate a sense of connection between the body and mind, promoting relaxation, and reducing stress.

Medication is another aspect that may need to be considered in some cases. Some PTSD symptoms can be alleviated with the help of medication, which can indirectly contribute to improved physical health. But it's important to remember that any medication use should be closely supervised by a healthcare professional.

Additionally, regular health check-ups can be instrumental in identifying any potential physical health issues early and implementing timely interventions. Being proactive about physical health can go a long way in maintaining overall wellbeing while managing PTSD.

Ultimately, understanding the connection between PTSD and physical health underscores the importance of holistic care in the journey towards recovery. By taking care of the body as well as the mind, individuals dealing with PTSD can better equip themselves to navigate the choppy seas of this condition, and work towards a future where they are not just surviving, but truly thriving.

So, while the interplay between PTSD and physical health can indeed add another layer of complexity to this condition, it also opens up new avenues for care and recovery. With comprehensive, compassionate care that encompasses both the psychological and physical realms, individuals with PTSD can not only manage their symptoms, but also protect and enhance their overall health and wellbeing.

Chapter 6: The Role of Resilience

There are waves in the ocean that toss the strongest ships, leaving them adrift and directionless. Similarly, the storms of our lives, like PTSD, can often lead us into a sea of despair. It's during these times that resilience emerges as our true compass, pointing us towards the shores of recovery.

Resilience is the ability to bounce back from adversity. It's about standing tall even when the world is pulling you down, about finding a way out even when you're enclosed by walls of despair. It is a powerful trait, a mental strength that shines brightest in times of crisis, guiding us towards hope and healing.

In the context of PTSD, resilience plays a pivotal role. The turbulent waves of this condition can be relentless, but resilience equips us with the power to confront these choppy seas. It encourages us to stare trauma in the face and say, "I will not be defeated."

But how do we cultivate this resilience? How do we nurture this capacity within ourselves to bounce back from the adversities that PTSD brings? It's important to remember that resilience isn't a fixed trait; it's more like a muscle. With consistent practice and the right resources, we can learn to strengthen this muscle, making us more equipped to navigate the challenging seas of PTSD.

In this chapter, we will explore the concept of resilience, delve into ways of building it, and understand its role in PTSD recovery. We'll provide strategies and tools to foster resilience, highlighting how this powerful trait can serve as a beacon of hope and a lifeline during our journey of healing from PTSD.

Understanding Resilience

We've all marveled at the resilience of a tree bending under the fierce gales of a storm, only to bounce back when the winds cease. This powerful capacity is not only a characteristic of nature, but also an intrinsic part of us - humans. Resilience is that mental fortitude that empowers us to rise from the ashes of adversity, to endure, and grow stronger in the face of life's storms.

In essence, resilience is not the absence of adversity or trauma but the ability to navigate through it, to maintain equilibrium, and move forward in the face of hardship. Resilience is not immunity from pain, distress, or failure, but the capacity to continue to function effectively despite them. In the face of setbacks, resilient individuals can adapt, learn, and become stronger.

One might wonder if resilience is a trait that only a few are blessed with. Is it a trait that we're born with or something we can develop? The answer to this is both enlightening and empowering. While it's true that some people might have a natural tendency towards resilience due to their genetics or upbringing, resilience is not a fixed attribute. It's dynamic, fluid, and most importantly, learnable.

Think of resilience as a collection of skills, not a single, unchangeable trait. It's an amalgamation of behaviors, thoughts, and actions that can be learned and developed by anyone. It's about how you perceive and respond to stress and adversity. Do you perceive a situation as a catastrophe or as a challenge? Is it an insurmountable obstacle or an opportunity for growth? These perceptions shape our resilience.

For people dealing with PTSD, understanding, and fostering resilience can make a significant difference. PTSD is not a sign of weakness; it's a sign that you've been through something traumatic, something that shook you to your core. While the trauma was not your choice, your response to it can be. That response is where resilience comes into play.

Cultivating resilience doesn't mean that you won't have trouble or distress. People who have risen above adversity are not those who've never fallen but those who never give up. They understand that setbacks are part of life, not the end of it. Resilience gives us the strength to tackle the issue head-on, to acknowledge and understand it, and to seek help when needed.

Moreover, resilience is about fostering wellness in various domains of our lives. It's about establishing supportive relationships, maintaining physical wellness, developing emotional intelligence, and fostering a positive outlook. It's about adopting a solution-oriented mindset and cultivating coping mechanisms that work best for us.

In the context of PTSD, resilience can also involve acceptance. Not acceptance of the trauma, but acceptance of the fact that life has changed. It's about understanding that while you cannot change the past, you can control your response to it. You can choose healing, growth, and recovery.

Furthermore, resilience involves the understanding that healing is a journey, not a destination. It's about being patient with yourself and acknowledging that recovery takes time. It's about celebrating small victories and understanding that each step, no matter how small, is a step forward.

Resilience does not eliminate the struggles of life, but it does equip us with the strength to tackle them, to rise, to learn, and to move forward. It teaches us that we are not defined by our adversities, but by how we rise from them.

Understanding resilience, therefore, is the first step towards cultivating it. In the following sections, we'll focus on how to build and foster resilience, offering strategies and tools to help you navigate the choppy seas of PTSD. Just as a tree bends but doesn't break in a storm, know that you too possess this inherent strength. Remember, the same waters that seem tumultuous now, once calmly cradled you. You can find that calm again. You are more resilient than you believe.

Building Resilience

Building resilience is akin to weaving a lifeboat, one that can keep us afloat when the seas of life turn choppy. We collect materials, weave them together, strengthen them, and step by step, we construct something sturdy and reliable. In the same way, building resilience requires gathering tools, skills, and techniques that can be learned, practiced, and honed over time.

The first thread in this tapestry of resilience is the cultivation of positive relationships. We are social beings and having a strong support system can significantly impact our ability to bounce back from adversity. Reach out to those who make you feel understood and valued, whether they are family members, friends, coworkers, or members of support groups. Sharing your experiences and feelings with them can lighten your burden, provide comfort, and make you feel less isolated. Likewise, lend an ear to others and offer help when you can. Helping others can create a sense of purpose and improve your own resilience.

Physical wellness is another crucial aspect of building resilience. Our bodies and minds are intricately linked, and taking care of one often benefits the other. Regular physical activity, a balanced diet, and adequate rest can boost your energy, improve your mood, and enhance your overall sense of well-being. These in turn can increase your capacity to cope with stress and adversity.

Cultivating emotional intelligence is another critical tool for building resilience. Emotional intelligence involves recognizing, understanding, and managing our own emotions and those of others. By developing a better understanding of our emotions, we can respond to them more effectively rather than react impulsively. This allows us to handle stress more efficiently, empathize with others, and maintain healthier relationships, all of which contribute to resilience.

One of the key aspects of resilience is maintaining a positive outlook. This doesn't mean ignoring the reality of the situation, but rather choosing to focus on potential solutions rather than ruminating on the problems. Try to identify something positive in each day, no matter how small it may seem. Engage in activities you enjoy and find meaningful. These can lift your spirits and provide a break from stress, fostering resilience in the process.

Developing a solution-oriented mindset is another important step towards building resilience. When faced with a problem, instead of fixating on what is wrong, switch your focus to finding solutions. What can be done to improve the situation? What steps can you take to mitigate the impact of the problem? This shift in perspective can make problems seem less overwhelming and more manageable.

Practicing mindfulness and relaxation techniques, such as deep breathing, meditation, or yoga, can also bolster resilience. These practices can help you stay focused on the present moment, reducing negative thought patterns and enhancing your overall sense of peace and tranquility. This inner calmness can serve as a buffer against the stress and adversity that come with PTSD.

Finally, acceptance plays a vital role in building resilience. Acknowledge the reality of your situation without trying to change or deny it. This is not an act of surrender, but an act of courage. It's a necessary step towards managing the situation effectively.

Building resilience is a personal journey that takes time and practice. Remember, you don't need to do it all at once. Start with small steps. Every action you take towards building resilience is a testament to your strength and determination. It's a reaffirmation of your capacity to navigate through the stormy seas of PTSD and reach the calm shores of recovery. With each thread you weave into your tapestry of resilience, you become better equipped to manage the adversities that life throws your way. You have the power to build resilience, one step at a time.

The Role of Resilience in PTSD Recovery

As we have navigated through the concept of resilience and its building blocks, we now arrive at the heart of our journey: the role of resilience in the recovery from Post-Traumatic Stress Disorder (PTSD). The human spirit's capacity to rebound from adversity and maintain its will to move forward is remarkable. This indomitable quality, this resilience, serves as a lighthouse guiding us through the storm towards the land of healing and recovery.

Resilience as a Facilitator of Healing

The first role of resilience in PTSD recovery lies in its ability to act as a facilitator of healing. It serves as an inner force, inspiring us to seek help and employ strategies to manage PTSD symptoms effectively. By providing the strength to acknowledge the reality of our situation, resilience leads us on the path of healing.

Resilience as a Buffer Against Stress

Stress is a common companion of PTSD, but resilience can serve as a buffer, absorbing the shocks of life's adversities. Resilient individuals tend to have more robust coping mechanisms, enabling them to handle stress better. They can understand and regulate their emotions, view problems from various perspectives, and approach situations with a solution-oriented mindset. This buffering effect reduces the impact of stress, thereby aiding in PTSD recovery.

Resilience as a Source of Hope

Resilience shines brightly as a beacon of hope, reassuring us that despite the storm, calm seas lie ahead. It tells us that while PTSD is a part of our story, it does not define us. This sense of hope can invigorate us, providing the motivation to pursue treatment, practice self-care, and invest in relationships, all crucial components of PTSD recovery.

Resilience as a Reinforcer of Positive Relationships

Resilient individuals understand the importance of positive, supportive relationships in their recovery journey. They strive to build and maintain these relationships, which provide emotional support, help cope with stress, and contribute to a sense of belonging. These healthy relationships serve as pillars of strength, further reinforcing resilience and promoting recovery.

Resilience as a Promoter of Personal Growth

Resilience also plays a role in personal growth following trauma. It provides the strength to rise from adversity and the wisdom to learn from it. The experience of overcoming adversity can foster a sense of self-efficacy, reinforce personal values, and nurture empathy for others facing similar challenges. This post-traumatic growth can contribute significantly to recovery.

Resilience as a Builder of Self-Esteem

In PTSD recovery, resilience can help build self-esteem. By overcoming challenges, we not only enhance our resilience but also our belief in ourselves. This improved self-esteem can decrease feelings of helplessness, replace self-doubt with self-assurance, and fuel the drive towards recovery.

Resilience as a Facilitator of Acceptance

Finally, resilience aids in acceptance, an essential component of PTSD recovery. Acceptance here refers to understanding the reality of the present situation, recognizing our emotions, and acknowledging that change is a part of life. This acceptance is a significant step towards managing PTSD effectively and moving forward in the healing journey.

In essence, the role of resilience in PTSD recovery is multifaceted, serving as a facilitator of healing, a buffer against stress, a source of hope, a reinforcer of positive relationships, a promoter of personal growth, a builder of self-esteem, and a facilitator of acceptance. As we nurture and strengthen our resilience, we bolster our ability to navigate the recovery journey, bringing us closer to the shores of peace and healing. The seas we navigate may indeed be choppy, but with resilience as our compass, we can sail towards a brighter, healthier future.

Chapter 7: Diagnosis and Assessment of PTSD

As we continue our journey through the complex world of PTSD, it's essential to turn our attention to a critical aspect of this condition - the process of diagnosis and assessment. This is a cornerstone in any individual's journey through PTSD, whether it be for themselves or a loved one. Understanding this process can provide clarity about the steps involved, as well as alleviate any anxiety surrounding diagnosis.

PTSD can be an insidious condition. Its symptoms can manifest in many ways and can often be mistaken for other disorders, which can lead to misdiagnosis or delayed treatment. To accurately diagnose PTSD, mental health professionals rely on established criteria and a thorough assessment process.

It's important to remember that every individual's experience with PTSD is unique. The trauma endured, the resulting symptoms, and the impact on daily life can vary significantly from person to person. Thus, the diagnosis and assessment process aims to capture this individual experience accurately to tailor the most effective treatment plan.

In this chapter, we will walk you through the PTSD diagnostic criteria that clinicians use to identify the disorder. We'll shed light on what happens during the assessment process and the different tools used in it. Lastly, we'll discuss the importance of trauma screening, a step that often acts as the first move towards identification and treatment.

By understanding the process of diagnosing and assessing PTSD, you gain valuable insights into the journey towards recovery. It's a step that bridges the gap between understanding what PTSD is and the process of healing. It is through this understanding that we begin to shape the path towards a life that is not dominated by PTSD, but one where it is managed effectively.

PTSD Diagnostic Criteria

Understanding PTSD goes hand-in-hand with understanding its diagnostic criteria. These criteria are guidelines used by mental health professionals worldwide to determine whether someone is experiencing PTSD. They were developed through extensive research and clinical expertise and serve as a roadmap to identify and categorize symptoms.

The Diagnostic and Statistical Manual of Mental Disorders, 5th Edition (DSM-5), developed by the American Psychiatric Association, currently provides the leading guidelines for diagnosing PTSD. The DSM-5 lays out specific criteria that must be met for an individual to be diagnosed, which we'll explore in this section.

The first criterion (Criterion A) concerns the traumatic event that led to the onset of symptoms. For a PTSD diagnosis, the individual must have been exposed to actual or threatened death, serious injury, or sexual violence. This exposure could be direct, such as being the victim of a traumatic event or witnessing it in person. It could also be indirect, such as learning about a close family member or friend experiencing a traumatic event or being exposed to aversive details of a traumatic event, typically in the line of professional duties.

Following Criterion, A, the DSM-5 sets out four symptom clusters: intrusive symptoms (Criterion B), avoidance of stimuli related to the trauma (Criterion C), negative alterations in cognition and mood (Criterion D), and alterations in arousal and reactivity (Criterion E).

Criterion B, the intrusive symptoms, can include recurring, involuntary, and intrusive distressing memories of the event, traumatic nightmares, flashbacks, or intense distress or physical reactions to trauma reminders. The person may find themselves constantly reliving the event in some way.

Criterion C, avoidance, is characterized by an effort to avoid distressing memories, thoughts, feelings, or external reminders associated with the trauma. This can manifest as avoiding conversations about the event, places or people that remind them of it, or even avoiding thinking about the event itself.

Criterion D involves negative changes in thoughts and mood that can lead to a distorted sense of blame, estrangement from others, or a reduced interest in activities. This might also involve the inability to remember key aspects of the traumatic event or a persistently negative emotional state.

Criterion E, changes in arousal and reactivity, might include irritable behavior, angry outbursts, reckless or self-destructive behavior, hypervigilance, an exaggerated startle response, problems with concentration, or sleep disturbances.

To meet the DSM-5 criteria for PTSD, the individual must exhibit one or more symptoms from Criteria B, C, and E, and at least two symptoms from Criterion D. Furthermore, these symptoms should last for more than one month (Criterion F), cause significant distress or functional impairment (Criterion G), and cannot be attributed to the physiological effects of substances or another medical condition (Criterion H).

While these criteria may seem clinical and impersonal, they act as an essential tool for mental health professionals. They guide them in identifying PTSD and distinguishing it from other conditions that might share similar symptoms, like anxiety disorders or depression. Furthermore, it's important to remember that behind these criteria lie real, individual experiences, which are complex and multifaceted.

Being familiar with the PTSD diagnostic criteria helps demystify the diagnosis process. However, a PTSD diagnosis should always be made by a qualified mental health professional. While these criteria provide a general guide, they aren't intended for self-diagnosis. Each individual's experience with trauma is unique, and it's crucial to seek professional help if you suspect you or a loved one may have PTSD.

Understanding the diagnostic criteria is not just about obtaining a diagnosis - it's also a steppingstone towards recovery. It's the first step in comprehending what you're going through and setting out on the journey towards healing. Through recognizing and identifying these symptoms, individuals and their loved ones can better understand what they are experiencing, opening the door to compassion, support, and effective treatment.

Assessment Process

Navigating the complex landscape of mental health diagnoses can feel overwhelming. It's crucial to understand what to expect throughout the assessment process for PTSD to feel more prepared and in control. Let's take a step-by-step look at this process, keeping in mind that while these steps are generally common, variations may occur based on individual needs and the approaches of different healthcare providers.

The first step in the assessment process is typically an intake interview. This is a comprehensive conversation between the individual and the mental health professional, usually a psychiatrist, psychologist, or therapist. The goal of this interview is to gather a broad view of the person's life, including past and present circumstances, physical health, mental health history, family background, and specifically, details about any traumatic events and related symptoms.

The clinician will likely use the DSM-5 criteria as a guide to structure the conversation around trauma and its aftermath. They'll ask about the nature of the traumatic event(s) and explore each symptom category, including intrusive thoughts, avoidance behaviors, changes in mood and cognition, and alterations in arousal and reactivity. This initial conversation is crucial, providing the foundation upon which the rest of the assessment builds. It's important to answer these questions as openly and honestly as possible, knowing that it's okay to say if there are things, you're not ready to talk about.

Following the intake interview, the clinician may administer specific psychological assessments or tests. These instruments are designed to measure and categorize symptoms in a standardized way. They may include self-report questionnaires like the PTSD Checklist (PCL-5), or structured interviews conducted by the clinician, such as the Clinician-Administered PTSD Scale (CAPS-5).

The PCL-5, for instance, is a 20-item questionnaire that aligns with the DSM-5 criteria for PTSD. It asks individuals to rate how much they've been bothered by specific symptoms over the past month. The CAPS-5 is a more in-depth interview-style assessment that evaluates the frequency and intensity of PTSD symptoms.

These assessments are designed to provide objective data about your symptoms. They can help validate your experiences and give both you and your clinician a clearer picture of what you're dealing with. The results can guide treatment planning and act as a benchmark to measure progress over time.

In addition to these PTSD-specific measures, the clinician may use other assessments to evaluate the presence of comorbid conditions, such as depression, anxiety, or substance use disorders. This is important because PTSD often doesn't exist in isolation. Assessing and addressing these additional conditions can significantly impact the overall treatment plan.

The clinician will also consider your physical health as part of the assessment process. PTSD can have physical manifestations, and sometimes, its symptoms may be confused with those of other medical conditions. In some cases, the clinician may refer you to a medical doctor for a physical examination or further tests to rule out any underlying medical issues that might be contributing to your symptoms.

Once the clinician has gathered all this information, they will evaluate it in light of the diagnostic criteria for PTSD and other mental health disorders. This involves a careful, thoughtful review of your symptoms, their duration and impact on your life, and any other relevant factors. They will then share the diagnosis with you and discuss the next steps.

Being diagnosed with PTSD can stir up a mix of emotions. You might feel relief at having a name for your experience, coupled with fear or sadness about what it means. It's okay to feel all these things. It's also okay to ask questions, seek clarification, or express doubts if you have them.

Remember, the assessment process is not about labeling or stigmatizing you. It's about understanding what you're experiencing so that you can get the right kind of help. Having a diagnosis doesn't change who you are – it just means you now have a roadmap for your journey towards healing.

Trauma Screening

Screening for trauma is an essential first step in recognizing and addressing Post-Traumatic Stress Disorder (PTSD). This process involves identifying individuals who have experienced traumatic events and who may be showing early signs of trauma-related symptoms. Screening is often performed by health care providers, social workers, or other professionals working in settings where exposure to trauma is likely, but it may also be the first step taken in mental health clinics when individuals present with symptoms that suggest possible PTSD.

The trauma screening process starts with questions that aim to identify whether an individual has experienced a traumatic event. These questions may be broad, covering various types of traumatic events such as physical or sexual assault, natural disasters, serious accidents, or combat experiences. It's important for the person answering these questions to feel safe and not pressured to disclose more than they are comfortable with at this stage. The focus is on establishing whether a potentially traumatic event has occurred.

After determining the presence of a traumatic event, the screener will usually ask some additional questions to assess the presence of common trauma-related symptoms. These may include symptoms of re-experiencing the trauma (such as nightmares or flashbacks), avoidance behaviors, and symptoms of hyperarousal (such as feeling jittery or being easily startled).

A screening does not yield a diagnosis. Instead, it helps identify those individuals who may be at risk and who would benefit from a more thorough assessment. The goal is to catch potential cases early, preventing the further development of symptoms and speeding up the route to effective help and support.

There are several different trauma screening tools available, each with its own set of questions and scoring system. Some of these include the Primary Care PTSD Screen for DSM-5 (PC-PTSD-5), the Trauma Screening Questionnaire (TSQ), and the Short Screening Scale for DSM-5 PTSD. These are brief questionnaires that can be completed in a matter of minutes. The choice of which tool to use can depend on the specific setting and the professional's preference.

The PC-PTSD-5, for example, is a simple screening tool consisting of five "yes" or "no" questions. If a person answers "yes" to any three questions, it suggests they may be experiencing PTSD and should receive a full diagnostic assessment. It's worth noting that this tool is specifically designed to screen for PTSD, not all forms of trauma, and its aim is to identify those who would benefit from further assessment, rather than to make a diagnosis.

The TSQ, on the other hand, contains ten yes/no questions that cover the key symptoms of PTSD. It is a little more extensive than the PC-PTSD-5 but still relatively brief. A person who answers "yes" to six or more questions is considered to be showing significant symptoms of PTSD and should be referred for a full diagnostic assessment.

If the screening indicates that a full assessment is needed, the individual will be referred to a mental health professional who can conduct a thorough assessment and, if appropriate, make a diagnosis and recommend a treatment plan.

It's essential to note that trauma screening should be carried out with sensitivity and respect, acknowledging the potentially distressing nature of the questions. Everyone involved in this process must remember that behind each answer is a personal story of hardship and resilience. Each person's experience of trauma is unique, and it's crucial to approach this process with empathy, understanding, and a genuine desire to help.

Trauma screening may be the first step on the path towards recovery for many individuals. By identifying those who are showing signs of trauma-related symptoms and getting them the help, they need, we can start to reduce the impact of these traumatic events and support individuals in their journey towards healing and growth. In this context, screening for trauma isn't just a set of questions – it's a lifeline, a signpost pointing towards hope, understanding, and recovery.

Chapter 8: Conventional Treatments for PTSD

After a diagnosis of PTSD, the next logical question one might have is, "What can be done?" Thankfully, with advancements in mental health practices, a range of conventional treatments for PTSD have emerged that can provide relief, growth, and recovery. This chapter explores those avenues that have shown promise in managing and alleviating the symptoms of PTSD, supporting individuals on their journey toward healing.

We will discuss the benefits and techniques of psychotherapy, a broad category encompassing numerous therapeutic practices that have been shown to be beneficial in managing PTSD. The chapter will also cover medicinal treatments, an aspect of PTSD management that can supplement other therapy forms and provide additional help in controlling symptoms. Finally, we will touch on group therapy, an option that provides a unique and supportive environment for sharing experiences and coping strategies.

As you read this chapter, consider that these treatments represent not just hope, but a testament to the resilience of those dealing with PTSD. With these tools, healing and growth become achievable goals, not distant dreams. This chapter aims to equip you with knowledge, providing you a deeper understanding of PTSD and the paths available for its treatment.

Psychotherapy

Psychotherapy is often referred to as 'talking therapy.' It's a collaborative journey, where therapists and patients work together to understand and manage the mind's tumultuous seas. Within the realm of PTSD, psychotherapy offers a safe harbor - a place to confront traumatic memories and navigate through them towards healing. One form of psychotherapy that has shown significant benefits for people dealing with PTSD is Cognitive Behavioral Therapy (CBT). It's like providing a compass to someone lost in the woods. CBT equips individuals with techniques to reframe negative thought patterns, encouraging a healthier perception of their experiences. Essentially, it works on the principle that our thoughts influence our feelings, which in turn affects our behavior. Change the thought, and you change the emotional response.

Imagine a person who experienced a car accident and has since developed a deep-seated fear of driving. Their mind constantly replays the traumatic event, creating anxiety and dread at the mere thought of getting behind the wheel. In CBT, the therapist helps them identify these thoughts and fears, and then gently guides them in challenging these notions. Instead of viewing driving as a threat, they are taught to understand it as an everyday activity that, while having risks, can be conducted safely.

Another form of psychotherapy commonly used for PTSD is Exposure Therapy. This approach may seem a little daunting at first. Imagine being asked to confront your deepest fears. The idea is to gradually, and in a controlled environment, expose the individual to their traumatic memories or triggers. Over time, this repeated exposure can lessen the intensity of the fear and anxiety associated with the trauma.

In the case of the person who has developed a fear of driving after the accident, an exposure therapy session might involve sitting in a stationary car, or watching videos of people driving. As they become comfortable with these exercises, they might progress to short drives around a parking lot, and eventually, to driving on quiet roads.

The intention is not to rush or force progress, but to allow the person to take each step at their own pace, with each successful step serving to lessen the fear and anxiety related to driving.

Prolonged Exposure Therapy (PET) and Eye Movement Desensitization and Reprocessing (EMDR) are also part of the psychotherapy family used to treat PTSD. PET is akin to exposure therapy but involves the individual revisiting the traumatic event in their mind and narrating it to the therapist. It's a process of unburdening, a release of pent-up fear and anxiety. EMDR, on the other hand, involves the person recalling the traumatic event while the therapist guides their eye movements. The purpose of this is to change the way the memory is stored, making it less distressing.

Let's not forget the importance of the therapeutic relationship itself. The relationship between the person and their therapist is a powerful component of the healing journey. It's the warm, supportive hand of someone who understands, someone willing to walk alongside them through the storm. This bond can be incredibly healing in itself, creating a space of trust and understanding where healing can begin.

Psychotherapy, in its various forms, offers individuals dealing with PTSD a variety of paths towards healing. From equipping individuals with tools to reshape their thinking and reactions, to allowing them to confront and control their fears, it embodies the essence of hope, growth, and recovery. Whether it's the gentle guidance of CBT, the courage-building processes of exposure therapies, or the calming rhythm of EMDR, these therapies are like lighthouses shining through the fog, offering direction, solace, and the promise of safer shores.

Medication

Medication plays a significant role in the treatment landscape for PTSD, like a lifeline thrown out to those struggling in turbulent waters. This chapter does not intend to be an exhaustive pharmacological study, but rather an overview of the commonly used medications and their role in alleviating the distressing symptoms of PTSD.

Antidepressants are commonly prescribed in the management of PTSD. They are like gentle whispers in the ear, encouraging the mind to let go of its persistent anxieties and depressive thoughts. Selective serotonin reuptake inhibitors (SSRIs) and serotonin and norepinephrine reuptake inhibitors (SNRIs) are often the first port of call. Serotonin is a neurotransmitter, a chemical messenger in the brain, that plays a crucial role in mood regulation. By preventing the reuptake, or absorption, of serotonin, these medications increase the availability of this neurotransmitter in the brain, thus helping lift the individual's mood and decrease anxiety.

Imagine you are in a dark room, and you're searching for a switch to turn on the light. SSRIs and SNRIs are like finding that switch, casting a warm and calming glow into the darkness. Medications such as fluoxetine (Prozac), sertraline (Zoloft), and venlafaxine (Effexor) are examples of this class of medication.

Apart from SSRIs and SNRIs, other classes of antidepressants such as mirtazapine (Remeron) or the atypical antidepressant bupropion (Wellbutrin) may be employed. It's like having an array of different keys, each capable of opening the same lock, but through different mechanisms.

Anxiety associated with PTSD can be severe and crippling. Benzodiazepines, a class of medication known for their anxiolytic or anti-anxiety effects, are sometimes used in the short-term management of severe anxiety. Imagine your anxiety as a roaring fire, consuming everything in its path. Benzodiazepines are like a fire extinguisher, quickly and effectively dousing the flames. However, due to the risk of dependence, these are typically not the first choice for long-term management. Another crucial aspect of managing PTSD is addressing the disrupted sleep patterns and nightmares that many individuals experience. Prazosin, originally an antihypertensive medication, has shown promise in reducing nightmares and improving sleep quality. It's like a lullaby, soothing the restless mind and easing the individual into a peaceful slumber.

The journey of treating PTSD is a long one, and the path isn't always smooth. Individuals may react differently to different medications, and what works for one person may not necessarily work for another. It's a process of trial and adjustment, of finding the right medication, or combination of medications, that best helps each individual. It is a partnership between the individual and their doctor, a shared decision-making process to determine the most beneficial course of treatment.

The story of PTSD and medication is not a tale of a magical pill that miraculously makes all the pain and distress disappear. It's a story of aid, of providing relief and making the journey towards recovery a little less burdensome. Medication serves as a tool, a sturdy walking stick that provides support and balance to the individual as they navigate through towards the harbor or the healing docks. With each step, with each day, it offers the hope of a better tomorrow, a life where PTSD no longer controls the narrative.

Group Therapy

Picture a circle of chairs in a room bathed in the gentle light of empathy and understanding. In each chair sits an individual, unique in their experiences, yet united by a common thread - the journey of living with and healing from PTSD. This is the arena of group therapy, a therapeutic modality that has proven to be remarkably effective in the management of PTSD.

Group therapy is akin to a garden where stories of hope, courage, and resilience bloom. The flowers, though varied, grow from the same soil - the shared experience of trauma. In this garden, individuals come together, not only to heal but also to inspire and be inspired.

It operates under the guidance of one or more therapists, serving as the gardeners, gently tending to the needs of the group while facilitating discussion and shared learning. This therapeutic modality offers a multitude of benefits, the most prominent being the sense of community and shared understanding it cultivates.

Imagine the solitude of suffering, the feeling of being trapped in a bubble of despair. Group therapy pierces that bubble, allowing individuals to connect with others who understand their struggles. It's like finding a reflection of your own experiences in the stories of others, creating a sense of unity and camaraderie that can be deeply comforting.

Group therapy also allows individuals to learn from the experiences and coping strategies of others. Picture a tree in a storm, bending but not breaking under the force of the wind. In the same way, the members of the group share their own 'storms' and how they've learned to 'bend' - their methods for coping, their successes, and their challenges. This shared knowledge pool can be a potent source of ideas and strategies for managing PTSD symptoms.

Moreover, group therapy offers a safe space for individuals to express their feelings and fears without judgment. Like a sanctuary, it provides shelter and comfort, allowing individuals to voice their innermost thoughts and emotions. The process of sharing can be therapeutic in itself, acting as a release valve for pent-up feelings, reducing feelings of shame and isolation.

Groups can be structured in different ways. Some may follow a more structured approach, focusing on teaching coping skills or following a specific therapeutic modality such as cognitive-behavioral therapy. Others may be more supportive in nature, emphasizing shared experiences and mutual support. Just like different types of soil nurtures different kinds of plants, the type of group selected can cater to the specific needs and preferences of the individual.

The journey through group therapy is a shared voyage, a winding river that meanders through valleys of self-discovery, mountains of resilience, and plains of mutual support. It's not about erasing the past but learning to navigate the present and future with newfound strength and understanding. It's about realizing that one is not alone in their struggle, that there are others who understand, and together, they can help each other heal.

For many, group therapy becomes a lighthouse in the stormy seas of PTSD - a beacon of hope, of community, and of healing. Through this therapeutic process, individuals not only find help but often discover within themselves a wellspring of courage and resilience they never knew existed. The power of this shared journey, this shared healing, can truly be a transformative experience on the path to recovery from PTSD.

Chapter 9: Alternative Therapies for PTSD

Post-traumatic Stress Disorder (PTSD) can often be a complex condition to manage and overcome. While traditional therapies and medical treatments have proven effective, there's growing recognition of the benefits that alternative therapies can bring to the table. These therapies serve as additional tools that can supplement traditional treatments, enhancing the recovery process.

In this chapter, we are going to explore several alternative therapies that have shown potential in helping individuals manage PTSD symptoms and improve overall well-being. These therapies take a holistic approach, addressing not just the mind but also the body and spirit, thus facilitating comprehensive healing.

We will start our exploration with mindfulness and meditation, powerful practices that encourage presence, acceptance, and self-awareness. Then we'll move on to yoga and physical activity, which build bodily strength and foster mental clarity, proving helpful in mitigating symptoms of PTSD.

Lastly, we'll turn our attention to the creative arts—specifically art and music therapy. These therapeutic practices leverage the healing power of creativity, offering an avenue for self-expression and emotional release.

Please note that these therapies should not replace professional help but can act as beneficial supplementary treatments. As we navigate through this journey, remember, the most crucial step is to find what works best for you. Everyone's journey to recovery is unique, and the therapeutic practices that assist you might differ from those that help others. The goal is to uncover an individual path to healing that resonates with you and supports your unique needs and experiences.

Mindfulness and Meditation

Mindfulness and meditation, both ancient practices with deep roots in Eastern philosophy, have emerged in recent years as effective tools for managing mental health, including conditions like PTSD. But what exactly are these practices, and how do they help?

Mindfulness refers to a state of awareness, where one intentionally focuses on the present moment in a non-judgmental manner. It's about cultivating a consciousness that anchors us to the here and now, allowing us to engage fully with our current experiences.

Meditation, on the other hand, is a practice through which we train our mind and attention. It involves techniques that promote relaxation, build internal energy, and foster a sense of calm and clarity. It's an exercise of the mind, akin to how physical activity is an exercise for the body.

When used as tools for managing PTSD, mindfulness and meditation can provide a multitude of benefits:

Reducing Hyperarousal: One of the key symptoms of PTSD is a heightened state of arousal, often resulting in anxiety, irritability, and sleep disturbances. Mindfulness and meditation can help to calm this hyperactive state, promoting relaxation and easing tension.

Improving Emotional Regulation: By focusing on the present moment, mindfulness encourages us to confront our emotions instead of avoiding them. This increased awareness can help us understand and manage our emotional responses better, contributing to better emotional regulation.

Decreasing Rumination: PTSD can often lead to ruminative thinking, where one obsessively repeats distressing thoughts. Meditation, with its emphasis on clearing the mind and focusing on the present, can help reduce such ruminations.

Promoting Self-Compassion: Through the non-judgmental awareness fostered by mindfulness, we can cultivate greater self-compassion, recognizing our pain without criticism and treating ourselves with kindness and understanding.

Encouraging Acceptance: Mindfulness and meditation can help us accept our present situation, recognizing our emotions and thoughts without trying to change or avoid them. This acceptance can be a crucial step towards recovery.

To practice mindfulness, you might start by choosing a quiet location, setting a specific time, and focusing on your breath. Notice your thoughts and feelings without judgment, and when your mind wanders, gently guide it back to your breath.

Meditation can take many forms, from focused attention practices where you concentrate on a single point, to open-monitoring practices where you observe all aspects of your experience without judgment. Techniques such as guided imagery, where you visualize a peaceful scene or location, can also be beneficial.

Meditation can be as simple or as elaborate as suits your comfort level. Focused attention practices, as the name suggests, involve focusing on a single thing. This could be your breath, a word or phrase known as a mantra, or even the sensation of the ground beneath you. The goal is to build your capacity to maintain attention on a single point, teaching your mind to become still and focused. When your mind inevitably wanders, you gently, without judgment, bring your attention back to the point of focus.

Open-monitoring practices, on the other hand, take a broader scope. Instead of focusing on one point, you aim to observe all aspects of your experience without judgment or reaction. You may note your breath, thoughts, feelings, or sensations as they arise and pass away. The goal is not to get rid of thoughts or to empty the mind, but rather to simply watch them come and go without becoming entangled in them.

Guided imagery is another technique that you can employ. This method involves visualization to evoke relaxation. You might imagine a peaceful scene or location that brings you joy and serenity. As you visualize this tranquil place, your body begins to respond as if you were really there – your heart rate slows, your breathing deepens, and your muscles relax.

Mindfulness and meditation are not about 'emptying the mind' or achieving a state of eternal calm. Rather, they are tools for developing a different relationship with your thoughts and feelings. They allow you to create a space between yourself and your experiences, so you can observe your thoughts and feelings without becoming overwhelmed by them.

With PTSD, distressing memories or feelings can feel very immediate and intrusive. Practicing mindfulness and meditation can help you develop the ability to observe these experiences without being swept away by them. You can learn to notice distressing thoughts as just that - thoughts, rather than facts or commands that you must act on.

Yoga and Physical Activity

Yoga and physical activity serve as a bridge between the mind and the body. They offer therapeutic effects by focusing on the connection between physical health and mental well-being, making them valuable resources in the management of PTSD.

Yoga, a practice originating from ancient India, is much more than physical exercise. It encompasses breath control, simple meditation, and the adoption of specific bodily postures. Its emphasis on mind-body integration makes it an ideal practice for those dealing with PTSD.

A typical yoga session might include:

- Asanas (postures): These physical poses help build strength, flexibility, and balance. They can also help to reduce physical tension and promote relaxation. There are hundreds of asanas to choose from, so it's easy to find ones that suit your ability and comfort level. For instance, the "Mountain Pose" (Tadasana) can promote steadiness and groundedness, while the "Child's Pose" (Balasana) can offer a soothing sense of comfort and security.

- Pranayama (breathing exercises): Controlled breathing exercises can help regulate your body's stress response, promoting relaxation and reducing anxiety. An example is "Equal Breathing" (Sama Vritti), where you inhale and exhale for an equal length of time, encouraging balance and calm.

- Meditation and mindfulness: Many yoga sessions conclude with a period of relaxation or meditation. This practice can help you cultivate mindfulness, allowing you to be present in the moment without judgment.

Physical activity, too, plays a crucial role in managing PTSD. It can help to reduce anxiety, improve mood, and enhance overall mental health. Regular physical activity can also help to improve sleep, a common issue for those living with PTSD. The type of physical activity can vary greatly, and it's essential to choose something that you enjoy and that suits your fitness level. This could be anything from walking or swimming to cycling or dancing.

While the mental health benefits of yoga and physical activity are evident, their role in PTSD recovery goes deeper. Here's how:

- Body Awareness: Yoga and physical activity can help enhance body awareness, or the ability to pay attention to your body's sensations. This enhanced body awareness can help you to better recognize and respond to your stress signals.

- Emotional Regulation: By promoting relaxation and reducing stress, yoga and physical activity can contribute to better emotional regulation, helping you to manage the intense emotions often associated with PTSD.

- Grounding: Physical practices can help you to feel more grounded and present in the moment, countering the feelings of disconnection or dissociation that can occur with PTSD.

- Empowerment: Learning new yoga postures or meeting physical activity goals can boost your confidence and give you a sense of control, countering feelings of helplessness or fear.

- Social Connection: Group yoga classes or team sports provide an opportunity for social interaction, helping to counter feelings of isolation.

Adapting Yoga for PTSD Recovery

Yoga can be modified to cater to the individual needs of those managing PTSD. Trauma-sensitive yoga is a term used to describe yoga practices that are specifically designed to be safe and effective for individuals who have experienced trauma. These classes typically emphasize creating a comfortable, non-judgmental space. They provide options and encourage students to make choices about what feels right for their body, thus promoting a sense of empowerment.

- Choice: In trauma-sensitive yoga, it is important to always offer choices and invite individuals to listen to their body. They can then choose what feels safe and comfortable. This choice can be about physical poses, use of props, or even the decision to rest at any time.
- Safety: The yoga space is arranged to promote safety. This might involve ensuring that all participants can see the door, or that the class is structured in a way that avoids sudden loud noises or other potential triggers.
- Mindfulness: Incorporating mindfulness in trauma-sensitive yoga can help bring individuals back to the present moment, grounding them when they are dealing with flashbacks or distressing memories.

Incorporating Physical Activity

Physical activity as part of PTSD recovery is not about pushing the body to its limits, but rather about moving the body in ways that feel good and foster a sense of well-being.

- Setting Achievable Goals: It can be helpful to start with small, achievable goals. If you're new to exercise, this could be as simple as a ten-minute walk each day. Over time, as your fitness improves, you can gradually increase the intensity and duration of your physical activities.
- Choosing Enjoyable Activities: Physical activity should be something you enjoy, not a chore. If you love nature, activities like hiking or birdwatching can be a good fit. If you're more social, consider team sports or group exercise classes. The key is to find something you look forward to doing.
- Routine and Consistency: Establishing a routine can be beneficial. Regular physical activity can provide structure to your day, which can be comforting when dealing with the unpredictability of PTSD symptoms.

In summary, yoga and physical activity can play a vital role in the recovery process from PTSD. By promoting body awareness, aiding in emotional regulation, and providing opportunities for empowerment and connection, these practices offer a path to reclaim control over your life. They are not standalone treatments for PTSD but are valuable components of a comprehensive, multifaceted approach to recovery. Remember, it's crucial to consult with healthcare professionals and seek out trauma-sensitive fitness professionals to ensure the safety and effectiveness of your fitness journey.

Art and Music Therapy

Just as every word in a book contributes to the narrative's overall message, every brush stroke in a painting or every note in a melody can contribute to the journey of healing and recovery. Art and music therapy can play a significant role in the journey to overcome PTSD. They provide a creative outlet to express emotions and experiences, often helping individuals communicate feelings they find too difficult to put into words.

Art Therapy: The Canvas of Emotions

Art therapy can serve as a non-threatening way to confront and process traumatic memories. By engaging in the creative process, you are not just creating art; you are also creating a safe space to explore your feelings, thoughts, and experiences related to trauma. Here's how:

- Self-expression: Art therapy enables you to express your emotions and thoughts visually. It provides a language beyond words to communicate complex feelings associated with trauma.
- Creating a narrative: Through your art, you can create a narrative of your traumatic experiences. This process can help you make sense of your trauma and integrate it into your life story in a manageable way.
- Relaxation and stress relief: The act of creating art can also be calming and therapeutic. It helps shift focus from the traumatic experience to the process of creation, thereby providing a respite from painful memories and thoughts.
- Empowerment: By choosing what and how to create, you can regain a sense of control, often lost in traumatic experiences. This creative control can be empowering and healing.

- Music Therapy: Healing Notes

  Music therapy can be a soothing balm for the emotional wounds of trauma. It can facilitate emotional expression, reduce stress, and foster a sense of connection with self and others.

- Emotional expression: Music can evoke powerful emotions. Through music therapy, you can tap into these emotions and express feelings related to your trauma in a non-verbal way.

- Relaxation: Listening to or creating music can induce relaxation and reduce stress, providing a beneficial counterbalance to the heightened arousal often associated with PTSD.

- Catharsis: Playing a musical instrument or singing can offer an emotional release or catharsis. It can provide a healthy outlet for anger, frustration, or sorrow, thus aiding in emotional regulation.

- Group bonding: Music therapy sessions often occur in a group setting. Participating in a music therapy group can foster a sense of belonging and connection with others, helping combat feelings of isolation that often accompany PTSD.

Both art and music therapy offer a means to access and process difficult emotions associated with PTSD. They provide a way to confront traumatic experiences indirectly, reducing the potential for re-traumatization. It's important to remember, however, that engaging in art or music therapy should be done under the guidance of trained therapists who can provide a safe and supportive environment for this process.

The journey through the choppy seas of PTSD is unique for everyone. The therapies that work best will depend on your individual experiences, preferences, and needs. Art and music therapy are just two of the many potential routes to healing. They offer a chance to express, explore, and ultimately, to heal. As you navigate your recovery, you might discover that these forms of therapy resonate with you, providing solace, understanding, and hope amidst the struggle.

Chapter 10: Self-Care and Lifestyle Changes

As we sail through life's choppy seas, the care and upkeep of our vessel — our mind and body — becomes of utmost importance. Dealing with PTSD requires more than just therapeutic interventions and medication; it calls for a holistic approach that encompasses self-care and various lifestyle changes. This chapter explores this realm, demonstrating how nurturing your physical, emotional, and mental well-being can facilitate recovery and enhance resilience.

Self-care, as a concept, emphasizes the importance of prioritizing one's own health and wellness. It's not about being selfish; rather, it's about acknowledging that your needs matter. It's about recognizing that you have the right to take care of yourself before extending help to others. In the context of PTSD, self-care involves taking active steps to manage symptoms, reduce stress, and improve overall quality of life.

Likewise, lifestyle changes can play a pivotal role in managing PTSD. Implementing healthy habits can create a supportive environment for healing, offering a solid foundation for therapeutic interventions to take effect. These changes could include maintaining a balanced diet, ensuring regular physical activity, cultivating a consistent sleep routine, fostering positive social connections, and avoiding harmful substances.

It's crucial to remember that these steps are not an alternative to professional treatment, but rather they complement it. They equip you with the strength and resilience to face the challenges posed by PTSD and ensure that your journey towards recovery is set on a healthy, stable, and positive path. By nurturing yourself and making mindful lifestyle choices, you're not just surviving PTSD — you're moving towards thriving despite it.

In the coming sections, we'll discuss various self-care strategies and lifestyle changes in detail, guiding you towards understanding and implementing them in your life. But before we do, take a moment to appreciate the steps you've already taken. Acknowledge the courage it takes to confront PTSD and remember, this journey is not a race, but a step-by-step process, unique to every individual. And in this journey, self-care and healthy lifestyle changes are your steadfast companions, helping you navigate the turbulent waters of PTSD.

Healthy Sleep Habits

Imagine your mind is a ship, tirelessly battling the stormy seas of PTSD, maneuvering through high winds and powerful waves. At the end of each long day, this ship needs to dock at a calm harbor to repair and replenish before it sets sail again. That safe harbor is a good night's sleep. Sleep allows your mind to rest, recuperate, and restore energy, which is essential when you are working to overcome something as challenging as PTSD.

A peaceful sleep, however, might seem like a distant dream when you're dealing with PTSD. Nightmares, flashbacks, and the constant state of hyperarousal can disrupt sleep, making it difficult to achieve the restful state that your body and mind need. Therefore, cultivating healthy sleep habits is not just a part of self-care; it's an integral aspect of your recovery journey.

First, let's understand the importance of a good sleep routine. Sleep isn't just about 'switching off' for a few hours. It's a complex biological process where your body performs vital tasks like repairing cells, flushing out toxins, and consolidating memories. More importantly, during sleep, your brain processes emotional information, which plays a significant role in managing stress, anxiety, and emotional reactions - aspects directly related to PTSD.

So, how do we create a sleep-friendly environment and routine?

- Establish a Consistent Sleep Schedule: Regulating your body's internal clock or circadian rhythm can improve sleep quality significantly. Try going to bed and waking up at the same time every day, even on weekends. This consistency reinforces your body's sleep-wake cycle and can help promote better sleep.
- Create a Restful Environment: Turn your bedroom into a sleep haven. Ensure it is dark, quiet, cool, and comfortable. You might want to consider using earplugs, an eye mask, or a white noise machine. A quality mattress and comfortable pillows can also make a big difference.

- Limit Daytime Naps: Long naps can interfere with nighttime sleep. If you choose to nap, limit yourself to about 30 minutes and make it during the mid-afternoon.

- Physical Activity: Regular physical activity can help you fall asleep faster and enjoy deeper sleep. However, timing is essential. Try not to exercise close to bedtime as it might interfere with sleep.

- Be Mindful of What You Eat and Drink: Avoid large meals, caffeine, and alcohol close to bedtime. These can disrupt sleep and lead to discomfort during the night.

- Wind Down: A calming pre-sleep routine can signal your body that it's time to wind down and sleep. This routine can include activities such as reading, taking a warm bath, listening to calm music, or doing some gentle stretching exercises.

- Use Your Bed for Sleep Only: It's essential to associate your bed with sleep only. Avoid using your bed for work, eating, or watching TV. This helps your brain associate the bed with sleep and creates a clear distinction between activities that require alertness and sleep.

- Consider a Sleep Journal: Keeping a sleep journal can help identify patterns or issues that affect your sleep. Note down when you go to bed, wake up, how often you wake up during the night, and how rested you feel in the morning.

As you incorporate these strategies, remember that change takes time. Be patient with yourself. Some nights will be better than others. In fact, think of every night as a new journey. Some nights, the seas may be rough, and sleep may elude you. But other nights, the waters will be calm, and you'll dock smoothly into the harbor of restful sleep.

And on the nights when sleep doesn't come easily, instead of fighting it, acknowledge the struggle. Remind yourself that it's okay to have a difficult night and that tomorrow is another chance to try again. Over time, with consistent efforts, the restless nights will decrease, and peaceful sleep will become the norm.

When sleep improves, the days also get better. You wake up feeling refreshed, energetic, and more equipped to face the challenges of the day. The stormy seas become a little less daunting, and your ship, powered by the energy from a good night's sleep, is ready to continue its journey.

Diet and Nutrition

Picture your body as a complex, highly efficient machine. This machine requires a certain type of fuel to perform optimally and maintain its parts in good working condition. The fuel we refer to here is the food we eat – our diet, and the nutrients it provides.

Maintaining a healthy diet is an essential part of self-care and recovery, particularly for individuals with PTSD. The stress and anxiety associated with this condition often lead to irregular eating habits, such as skipping meals or overeating, both of which can have adverse effects on your physical and mental health. A balanced diet, on the other hand, provides your body with the necessary nutrients to manage stress better, improve mood, and enhance overall well-being.

The first step towards achieving a balanced diet is understanding the five main food groups: fruits, vegetables, grains, protein, and dairy. The key here is variety. Eating a mixture of these food groups ensures you're getting a wide array of essential nutrients.

Fruits and Vegetables: Strive to fill half your plate with fruits and vegetables at each meal. They are packed with vitamins, minerals, and fiber, helping you feel full and nourished. Opt for a colorful variety as different colors provide different nutrients.

Grains: Choose whole grains such as brown rice, whole wheat bread, and oatmeal, which provide sustained energy and are a good source of fiber.

Protein: Protein helps in building and repairing body tissues. Choose lean meats, poultry, fish, beans, eggs, and nuts.

Dairy: Opt for low-fat or non-fat dairy products, which provide you with necessary calcium and vitamin D.

Now that we have the basics covered, let's explore specific dietary practices that can aid in managing PTSD symptoms:

- Regular, Balanced Meals: Regular meals help stabilize blood sugar levels, affecting your mood and energy. Each meal should have a balance of protein, fat, and carbohydrates to ensure a steady release of energy.

- Hydrate: Water is essential for all bodily functions, including digestion and maintaining body temperature. Dehydration can lead to fatigue and irritability. Aim for at least 8 cups of water a day, more if you're active or in hot weather.

- Limit Caffeine and Sugar: While they provide a quick energy boost, the crash that follows can leave you feeling tired and irritable. They can also interfere with sleep, which is vital in managing PTSD symptoms.

- Omega-3 Fatty Acids: Research has shown Omega-3 fatty acids, found in fatty fish, flaxseeds, and walnuts, have mood-stabilizing effects and can help manage anxiety and depression.

- Vitamins and Minerals: B vitamins, particularly B6, B12, and folate, help in the production of neurotransmitters that regulate mood. Zinc, Magnesium, and Vitamin D also play crucial roles in maintaining mental health.

- Prebiotics and Probiotics: These support gut health, which is directly linked with mental health. Foods like yogurt, sauerkraut, and other fermented foods are rich in these.

As you incorporate these dietary practices, remember to be patient with yourself. Changing eating habits can be a slow process, and it's okay to take small steps. Each meal is a new opportunity to nourish your body and mind.

Imagine, if you will, a garden. A garden teeming with a variety of plants – colorful flowers, lush green shrubs, towering trees, each plant representing a part of your body, your mind, your spirit. The food you eat is like the water, the sunlight, the nutrients that you provide to this garden. The better the quality of these inputs, the healthier and more vibrant your garden will be.

Eating right is not about strict dietary limitations, staying unrealistically thin, or depriving yourself of the foods you love. Rather, it's about feeling great, having more energy, improving your health, and boosting your mood. Your journey to healing is not just about managing symptoms but also about rediscovering and nurturing yourself. It's about turning that tumultuous sea into a serene, peaceful garden. And the food you eat can be a powerful tool in this transformation.

Exercise and Movement

Imagine for a moment standing at the edge of a forest, ready to take a step into the unknown. The cool air brushes against your skin, the rustling of leaves whispers in your ears, and the earthy scent of the woods fills your lungs. As you begin to move, with each step, you become more aware of the world around you and more connected with yourself. This is what physical exercise, in essence, can do for your mind and body. It brings you to the present moment, connects you with your inner self, and ignites a spark of vitality and life within you.

Exercise, simply put, is any movement that makes your muscles work and requires your body to burn calories. It's a vital part of a healthy lifestyle and even more so in the management and recovery from PTSD. The physical benefits of exercise - weight control, reduced risk of chronic diseases, strengthened muscles and bones - are well known. But the mental health benefits are just as compelling.

Physical activity stimulates various brain chemicals that can leave you feeling happier, more relaxed, and less anxious. You may also feel better about your appearance and yourself when you exercise regularly, boosting your self-esteem and improving your sense of worth. But perhaps one of the most potent effects of exercise is on stress - it is a powerful stress buster.

Moving your body, be it a brisk walk in the park, a vigorous dance session, or a tranquil yoga practice, triggers a series of physiological responses. Your heart rate increases, your muscles work harder, and your breathing rate goes up. This physical response activates a relaxation response in the brain, helping to break the cycle of stress and anxiety characteristic of PTSD.

There are numerous ways to incorporate physical activity into your life. Here are a few suggestions:

- Cardiovascular exercises: Also known as cardio or aerobic exercises, these involve large muscle groups and increase your heart rate. Walking, jogging, swimming, and cycling are excellent examples. They not only improve your physical stamina but also have mood-boosting effects.

- Strength training: Activities like weightlifting or resistance band exercises help build muscle mass and strengthen your body. They also increase your metabolic rate, helping with weight control.

- Flexibility and balance exercises: Yoga, Tai chi, and Pilates improve your body's flexibility and balance. These activities also have a meditative quality to them, promoting mental tranquility.

- Mind-body exercises: These include practices such as Qigong and Tai Chi, which combine movement, meditation, and breathing exercises. They're designed to enhance physical health and mental well-being.

- Daily physical activity: Incorporate movement into your day-to-day life. Take the stairs instead of the elevator, walk to the nearby grocery store, play with your kids or pets. Small actions can add up to big health benefits over time.

When starting a new exercise regimen, it's important to set realistic goals. Start small, maybe a 10-minute walk around the block, and gradually increase the intensity and duration of your workouts. Listen to your body and avoid pushing yourself too hard too soon.

Remember the forest you stepped into earlier? With exercise, each step you take into this forest takes you deeper into a place of healing and recovery. Each movement is a conscious choice to take control of your life and reclaim your health. It's not always an easy path. You may stumble, lose your way, but with persistence and patience, you can navigate through this forest and emerge on the other side, stronger, healthier, and in control.

Exercise, like all lifestyle changes, requires consistency and commitment. But unlike some other forms of treatment, exercise comes with no side effects, only benefits. So, put on your walking shoes, unroll that yoga mat, and take that step. Your journey to recovery begins with movement.

Chapter 11: Support Networks

Living with PTSD can often feel isolating, but you are not alone in your journey towards recovery. One of the pillars that can greatly influence your healing process is your support network. These are the people who stand by you, offering emotional and practical help when you need it most.

A support network can include friends, family, mental health professionals, support groups, online communities, and anyone else who provides a sense of comfort and understanding. These individuals can help create a safe space where you can express your feelings without fear of judgment. They can provide encouragement, remind you of your strengths, and stand as a testament to the fact that you are cared for and valued.

Engaging with your support network can be an instrumental part of managing your PTSD symptoms. Regular contact with loved ones can help to mitigate feelings of isolation and provide a much-needed distraction from distressing thoughts and feelings. You might also find it helpful to share your experiences with others who have been through similar experiences, such as in a support group or online forum.

But it's not just about receiving support. Giving it can also be a powerful healing tool. Helping others, whether by lending a listening ear or providing advice, can foster a sense of purpose and boost your self-esteem.

Remember, it's okay to lean on others when you need to - it doesn't make you weak. It's a sign that you are taking proactive steps to manage your PTSD. It's about recognizing that we are social beings, and connection with others can be a source of great strength and resilience.

A support network won't make your PTSD disappear, but it can make the journey a bit less daunting. It's like having companions in a storm - they may not be able to stop the rain, but they can offer you an umbrella when you need it most.

Family and Friends

Among your support networks, family and friends often form the bedrock. These are the people who know you the most intimately, who have shared in your joys and sorrows, and who have a vested interest in your wellbeing.

Let's consider a story of Mark, a veteran diagnosed with PTSD. When he returned home after his service, he was a changed man. He struggled with nightmares, unexpected bouts of anger, and a general sense of unease. It was his sister, Laura, who first suggested he might be dealing with PTSD. Having noticed the changes in Mark's behavior, she encouraged him to seek professional help. Laura's support didn't stop there. She made it a point to educate herself about PTSD, its symptoms, and its impact.

And so, when Mark was finally diagnosed, Laura was there, ready to support him. She learned how to create a calming environment for Mark, reducing potential triggers at home. She was patient, listening to him when he was ready to talk, and giving him space when he needed it. Laura became an essential part of Mark's support system, and her understanding and acceptance played a significant role in his journey towards recovery.

This story illustrates the power of supportive family and friends in the life of a person dealing with PTSD. It isn't always easy, and it requires a lot of patience, empathy, and learning. But the role these individuals can play is invaluable.

So, how can family and friends be supportive? Firstly, by educating themselves about PTSD - its causes, symptoms, and effects. Knowledge will lead to better understanding, reduced stigmatization, and more effective support. Secondly, by being patient. Recovery takes time, and there might be setbacks along the way. Being a steady, patient presence can offer immense comfort. Lastly, by encouraging professional help and being an active part of the recovery process. This could involve accompanying your loved one to therapy sessions, if they're comfortable with it, or helping to implement coping strategies at home.

Having supportive friends and family can also lead to a greater feeling of self-worth and belonging, which are essential components for recovery. Positive social interactions can boost mood, reduce feelings of isolation, and provide distraction from distressing memories or thoughts.

It's equally important to note that supporting a loved one with PTSD can be challenging, and self-care should not be neglected. Remember to take breaks, seek support for yourself, and engage in activities that you enjoy. Supporting a loved one with PTSD is a team effort, and taking care of your mental health is just as important.

As family and friends, your understanding, patience, and support can act as a lifeline for someone dealing with PTSD. It's about being a safe harbor in their choppy seas, a place where they can find respite and regain their strength. Your role is not to fix them or to make the PTSD go away, but to stand by them, offering your support and love as they navigate their journey towards recovery.

Online Communities

In the modern age, the internet has opened doors to various resources, one of which is the possibility of joining online communities. These digital spaces can provide invaluable support to those dealing with PTSD, offering a platform to share experiences, learn from others, and realize that they are not alone in their struggles.

Let's consider the story of Naomi, a survivor of childhood trauma. She had always struggled with feelings of fear and anxiety, with nightmares that took her back to her traumatic past. But she wasn't comfortable sharing her experiences with her friends or family, fearing their judgment or a lack of understanding.

It was then that she discovered an online forum for trauma survivors. Here was a space where she could anonymously share her thoughts, fears, and experiences. She was met with empathy and understanding from others who had walked the same path. Here, Naomi wasn't alone.

Reading about others' experiences gave her insights into her own struggles. The coping strategies that worked for them, the resources they found helpful, all provided Naomi with new ways to manage her symptoms. It was one of these online friends who suggested she try trauma-focused cognitive behavioral therapy. Naomi followed up on this advice and found it to be extremely beneficial in her recovery process.

The story of Naomi illustrates the potential benefits of online communities for those dealing with PTSD. They can act as a safe, non-judgmental space for sharing experiences and finding support. They can also provide access to a wealth of resources and coping strategies, often shared by those who have found them useful in their own recovery journey.

But how can you find the right online community for you? Start by looking for forums, social media groups, or websites dedicated to mental health, PTSD, or trauma recovery. You could also ask your healthcare provider for recommendations. Once you've found a potential community, take some time to observe the interactions and discussions. Ensure that the community feels respectful, supportive, and moderated to maintain a positive environment.

Remember, though, online communities should not replace professional help. While they can offer support and understanding, it's essential to continue seeking professional treatment for PTSD.

Also, it's crucial to safeguard your online privacy. Use an anonymous username if needed, and avoid sharing personal details that could identify you.

Lastly, remember to be respectful of others' experiences and opinions in these communities. Everyone's journey with PTSD is different, and what works for one might not work for another.

Navigating PTSD can feel like sailing through choppy waters. The journey can be challenging and isolating, but the right support network can act as a beacon, guiding you towards safer shores. And sometimes, that beacon could be a supportive message from an understanding stranger in an online community. Even in the vast expanse of the digital world, you are not alone.

Professional Support Groups

Professional support groups offer a structured environment for individuals struggling with similar issues, such as PTSD, to come together under the guidance of a trained professional. These meetings can be powerful platforms for healing and recovery, providing both a sense of community and professional expertise.

Consider the journey of a woman named Ava. After a traumatic event, Ava was struggling with PTSD symptoms. She felt isolated and misunderstood by her friends and family who, despite their best intentions, found it difficult to fully comprehend what she was going through. One day, her therapist recommended she join a professional support group for individuals coping with trauma.

Despite her initial hesitation, Ava decided to give it a try. The first few meetings were difficult; Ava was not accustomed to opening up about her experiences. But she saw how others in the group, who were further along in their recovery, shared their stories with courage and honesty, and she felt encouraged to do the same.

Over time, the support group became a place of healing for Ava. It was a space where she felt understood, a place where her experiences were validated. Listening to the others share their journeys, their triumphs and setbacks, made Ava feel less alone in her own struggle. And as she began to share her story, she found a sense of release and understanding that she hadn't experienced before.

The group was facilitated by a trained professional who ensured the discussions remained respectful and supportive. They provided coping strategies, exercises, and resources that complemented Ava's individual therapy. Their expertise added an essential layer of guidance to the group's collective wisdom.

Ava's story underlines the potential benefits of joining a professional support group. In such a setting, not only can you find understanding and camaraderie among individuals facing similar struggles, but also receive guidance from a trained professional.

A professional support group can be a great complement to individual therapy. You can gain insights from others' experiences, learn new coping strategies, and build a network of support. It can also be a safe space to practice social interactions and communication skills that might have been affected by PTSD.

To find a professional support group, you can ask for recommendations from your healthcare provider, local mental health clinics, or online directories for mental health services. It might take a few tries to find the right fit, but don't get disheartened. Finding the right group, where you feel safe and supported, can be a key component of your recovery process.

However, remember that professional support groups are not a substitute for one-on-one therapy. It's crucial to continue with individual treatment even if you are part of a support group.

Professional support groups can serve as an additional source of strength and comfort, offering a sense of community and expert guidance. Participating in a group can make you realize that, even though the journey through PTSD can be challenging, you are not alone, and recovery is within your reach.

Chapter 12: PTSD and the Workplace

In the quiet hum of an office, amidst the shuffle of papers, clatter of keyboards, and murmur of conversation, there is an invisible struggle that many may not recognize - the silent fight against Post-Traumatic Stress Disorder (PTSD). The workplace, a significant part of our lives, often remains untouched in conversations about PTSD. However, trauma doesn't recognize boundaries, and its effects can seep into every facet of an individual's life, including their professional sphere.

The reality of PTSD in the workplace is layered and complex. It encapsulates both the challenges faced by those struggling with the disorder and the steps organizations can take to support them. This hidden issue needs more light, as it affects not only the individual but also the collective team and overall organizational performance.

In this chapter, we will explore the multifaceted nature of PTSD in the workplace, beginning with how PTSD can affect job performance and the interpersonal dynamics at work. We will then investigate the importance of understanding and acknowledging this issue within the professional environment.

Employers and co-workers often constitute a critical part of an individual's support network. As such, a workplace that fosters understanding and encourages supportive behavior can significantly aid an individual's healing journey. A well-informed workplace can be a pillar of support for those grappling with PTSD, as it promotes acceptance and mitigates the stigma often associated with mental health issues.

Through this exploration, we hope to encourage more inclusive, understanding, and supportive workplaces that recognize the reality of PTSD and are equipped to provide the necessary support. As we venture into this discussion, it's important to remember that every step towards understanding and empathy makes a significant difference in the journey of those living with PTSD.

Disclosure and Stigma

Opening up about mental health struggles, particularly in a professional setting, can often feel like navigating a minefield. On the one hand, there's the inner urge to share one's story, a desire to be authentic, and the practical necessity for some accommodations or understanding.

On the other hand, there's the fear of being judged, misunderstood, or even penalized. This balance is particularly delicate in the context of Post-Traumatic Stress Disorder (PTSD), a condition that is often laden with stigma and misunderstanding.

The decision to disclose PTSD to employers or colleagues is a deeply personal one. It depends on various factors, including the nature of the job, the severity of symptoms, the level of trust in the workplace, and personal comfort with disclosure. At its core, it's a choice about vulnerability, a step towards inviting others into a personal battle against trauma and its aftermath.

Stigma can be a significant barrier in this journey. Negative stereotypes about PTSD can breed misunderstanding and lead to prejudiced attitudes. It's not uncommon for individuals with PTSD to fear judgment or exclusion at their workplace. This fear can deter them from seeking necessary support and accommodations, hindering their healing process and reducing their job satisfaction and performance.

However, while stigma can feel like an insurmountable wall, it's crucial to remember that it thrives on ignorance and misunderstanding. Information and awareness can slowly chip away at this barrier, creating a more inclusive and empathetic environment. The more we talk about PTSD, the more we understand it, the easier it becomes to dispel misconceptions and foster a supportive workplace culture. Organizations can play a vital role in reducing stigma by promoting mental health awareness and creating policies that encourage openness. Anti-stigma programs, mental health trainings, and clear policies about mental health disclosure and accommodations can send a strong message to employees about the organization's commitment to their mental wellbeing. These actions can help foster a safe space for individuals to disclose their struggles and seek necessary support.

In an ideal world, the fear of stigma should never be a barrier to seeking support. However, we live in a world that's far from perfect. While we strive to reduce stigma, it's also essential to consider strategies for individuals who choose to disclose their struggles with PTSD. One crucial strategy is equipping individuals with the tools to communicate effectively about their condition. This includes knowing their rights, understanding what accommodations they might need, and how to request them, and being prepared for possible reactions.

Another strategy is building a supportive network within the workplace. This could be a trusted supervisor, a supportive HR representative, or a colleague who understands the struggle. This network can provide immediate support and act as an ally during challenging times.

While disclosure can be a daunting decision, it can also be a step towards creating a more understanding and supportive environment. In turn, this can improve not only the mental health of the individual with PTSD but also the overall health of the organization. Through understanding and empathy, we can transform professional environments into spaces that respect and nurture the mental wellbeing of all employees.

As we journey through this discussion, let us remind ourselves that every step we take towards understanding, every effort to reduce stigma, brings us closer to a world where no one has to fight their battles in silence.

Accommodations and Rights

Taking the step to disclose a PTSD diagnosis in the workplace signifies a pivotal point in one's journey of healing and acceptance. However, it's just the first step. Understanding one's rights and the possible accommodations that workplaces can provide is essential to making this disclosure truly beneficial.

Every individual with PTSD has a unique experience of the disorder. The impact on their work life can vary greatly depending on the severity and nature of their symptoms. As such, the accommodations needed for each individual can be quite diverse. However, there are some common accommodations that many people with PTSD may find helpful.

Some may benefit from a flexible schedule that allows them to attend therapy or medical appointments. Others may require a quiet workspace to reduce anxiety and distraction, or frequent breaks to manage fatigue and stress. Additional training, written instructions, or even changes in supervisory methods might be beneficial for those who struggle with memory or concentration.

To facilitate these accommodations, it's crucial for individuals with PTSD to understand their rights under the law. In many countries, legislation exists to protect the rights of people with disabilities, including mental health conditions like PTSD. For instance, in the United States, the Americans with Disabilities Act (ADA) requires employers to provide reasonable accommodations to qualified employees with disabilities, unless doing so would cause undue hardship to the employer.

A reasonable accommodation is any change in the work environment, or the way tasks are usually done that helps an individual with a disability apply for a job, perform job duties, or enjoy the benefits and privileges of employment. It's important to note that the employer has the discretion to choose among effective accommodations and does not have to provide the exact accommodation requested.

However, to access these rights, an individual must disclose their condition to their employer. The process of requesting accommodations usually involves a simple written request to the employer or HR representative, describing the nature of the disability, how it affects work performance, and suggesting possible accommodations.

It's crucial to note that the law also protects employees from discrimination based on their disability. This includes adverse actions related to hiring, firing, pay, job assignments, promotions, layoff, training, benefits, or any other term or condition of employment. Retaliation against an individual for asserting their rights under these laws is also prohibited.

Understanding one's rights and possible accommodations can empower individuals with PTSD to advocate for themselves in the workplace. It can help create a work environment that supports their mental health and facilitates their healing journey.

As we explore these rights and accommodations, it's important to acknowledge the role of employers in this process. A supportive and understanding employer can make a world of difference in the journey of an individual with PTSD. Employers who prioritize mental health, who are open to accommodations, and who foster an inclusive work environment can transform workplaces into safe havens rather than stressors.

Creating such a workplace is not just about complying with the law; it's about cultivating a culture of understanding, empathy, and respect. It's about acknowledging the human behind the employee, understanding their struggles, and supporting their journey. This culture benefits not just individuals with PTSD, but every employee in the organization, making the workplace a truly healthy and supportive environment.

In this dialogue about PTSD and the workplace, let's celebrate every employer who fosters such an environment, every colleague who offers understanding, and every individual who bravely discloses their struggle. Together, we can change the narrative around mental health in the workplace, making it a space that supports healing, understanding, and growth.

Balancing Work and Recovery

Every individual's journey to recovery from PTSD is uniquely their own, shaped by their experiences, their resilience, and the support they receive. One of the challenges often encountered on this road to recovery is finding the equilibrium between managing a career and focusing on healing. This balancing act requires understanding, patience, and adaptability.

For those grappling with PTSD, work can serve multiple purposes. It can offer a sense of routine and normalcy, providing a structured environment that can be comforting. Work can also serve as a distraction, a means to channel energy and focus away from traumatic memories. Yet, work also comes with its own set of stresses and demands that can exacerbate PTSD symptoms. Recognizing this delicate interplay is the first step towards balancing work and recovery.

One of the key components in striking this balance is self-awareness. Understanding one's triggers, recognizing signs of stress, and knowing when to step back is crucial. Being aware of what one can realistically handle and setting boundaries accordingly can prevent burnout and further trauma. It's important to remember that it's okay to take a step back when needed. Your health is your top priority.

Another component is flexibility. This can mean flexibility in one's work schedule to accommodate therapy sessions, or the flexibility to work remotely when the office environment becomes too overwhelming. Flexibility can also mean being open to changes in one's career trajectory. One might consider shifting to less stressful job roles or even exploring different career paths that could be more conducive to their healing.

Communication is equally important in this balancing act. This includes communicating with one's employer about necessary accommodations, communicating with one's therapist about work stresses, and equally crucial, communicating with oneself – acknowledging one's feelings and experiences without judgment.

The role of support systems can't be overstated when balancing work and recovery. Support can come in various forms, from understanding supervisors and colleagues, to professional mental health support, to online communities and support groups. These networks can offer advice, provide understanding, and help individuals feel less isolated in their experiences.

For example, consider Jake, a high school teacher who was diagnosed with PTSD. For Jake, the noise and chaos of a school day were overwhelming, causing heightened anxiety and distress. But he loved teaching and didn't want to give up his career.

Recognizing his struggles, Jake requested a reasonable accommodation under the ADA to allow him a quieter workspace for grading and planning. He also found a supportive online community of teachers managing mental health conditions, where he could share his experiences and learn from others. Additionally, he worked with his therapist to develop coping strategies for his workday, such as taking short breaks when he felt overwhelmed, practicing mindfulness exercises, and maintaining a consistent sleep routine to better manage fatigue. With these changes, Jake found that he was able to continue teaching while also prioritizing his recovery.

Jake's story illustrates the potential of finding this balance between work and recovery. It's a process of trial and error, of understanding and adjusting, of advocating and adapting. It's a journey that's not always easy, but it's one that's worthwhile.

At the heart of this balance is the recognition that recovery doesn't mean one has to put their life on hold. It's about integrating recovery into one's life in a way that allows for healing while also continuing to live, work, and grow. After all, recovery isn't just about overcoming trauma; it's about building a life beyond it, a life defined not by trauma but by resilience and hope.

Chapter 13: PTSD in Veterans

War zones are breeding grounds for trauma. Our brave men and women in uniform are exposed to circumstances that most of us can't even imagine. It's not just the fear of combat that's nerve-wracking; it's also witnessing tragedies, seeing friends hurt or worse, and the constant anticipation of danger that can take a toll on their mental health. One of the most common conditions that veterans face when they return home is Post-Traumatic Stress Disorder, or PTSD.

Every veteran's experience with PTSD is unique, reflecting the individual's personal resilience, the nature of the traumatic event, and the support system they have in place. But commonly, these courageous individuals find themselves grappling with flashbacks of traumatic experiences, hyper-vigilance, sleepless nights, and an overwhelming sense of anxiety. They may feel emotionally numb, detached from loved ones, and struggle with feelings of guilt, shame, or self-blame.

PTSD can make transitioning back to civilian life a daunting challenge. Simple everyday tasks can trigger traumatic memories, making it difficult for veterans to reintegrate into society. The sounds of traffic might remind them of gunfire; a crowded room can bring back the panic of a battlefield. Even the joyous hug of a loved one might feel constraining, as if they're trapped.

For veterans, understanding and acknowledging that they're experiencing PTSD is the first step on their path to recovery. PTSD is not a sign of weakness; it is a normal reaction to abnormal events. It's important to remember that it's okay to ask for help and seek professional assistance when needed.

This chapter aims to bring you closer to understanding PTSD as it manifests in veterans. It's a difficult journey they tread, but with the right tools, strategies, and support, it is possible to navigate through the choppy seas of PTSD. By understanding their struggle, we can stand by them in their journey towards a life of peace and tranquility.

The Unique Challenges of Veterans

Serving in the military exposes individuals to experiences far removed from what most of us encounter in our daily lives. For veterans, their time in the military and the transition back to civilian life can come with a unique set of challenges. Let's explore some of these challenges more extensively:

The Trauma of Combat: The very nature of war puts soldiers in situations of extreme stress and life-threatening danger. Experiencing or witnessing violence, death, and destruction can lead to lasting mental health impacts, including PTSD. Combat veterans often grapple with intense flashbacks, intrusive memories, and nightmares that can disrupt their daily life.

Transition to Civilian Life: Reintegrating into civilian society after active service is a significant task. The military is a distinct culture with its own rules, values, and lifestyle. Moving from this highly structured environment to civilian life, which lacks the same clear hierarchy and order, can be jarring and disorienting for many veterans.

Physical Injuries and Disabilities: Many veterans return home with injuries, some leading to permanent disabilities. These physical challenges not only affect their ability to function day-to-day but also contribute to mental health issues. Feelings of anger, frustration, or self-pity due to physical limitations can exacerbate PTSD symptoms.

Emotional Numbness: The harsh realities of warfare often make soldiers emotionally numb as a defense mechanism. Once they return home, this emotional withdrawal can persist, making it difficult for them to connect with loved ones and causing feelings of isolation.

Guilt and Moral Injury: Veterans may struggle with guilt over actions they had to take or things they witnessed during service. This is often referred to as "moral injury." They may feel shame or remorse, struggle with the meaning of their actions, or even question their self-worth, further complicating their PTSD experience.

Lack of Understanding and Stigma: There is often a lack of understanding in society about the issues veterans face, which can lead to stigma. This can make veterans feel misunderstood and reluctant to seek help for their mental health issues, fearing judgement or dismissal.

Difficulty Seeking Help: Many veterans feel that their pride, or their wish to appear strong, prevents them from seeking help. This can be particularly true for those from military cultures that value self-reliance and toughness, making it even more challenging for them to access the support they need.

Employment Challenges: Transitioning to civilian work can be difficult for veterans, especially if they're dealing with PTSD. They may find that their military skills don't directly translate to civilian jobs, and PTSD symptoms can make job interviews, concentration, and interactions with coworkers challenging.

Homelessness and Financial Instability: Unfortunately, some veterans face homelessness and financial instability upon returning home. The struggle to secure stable employment can lead to financial difficulties, and PTSD can make it even harder to maintain stable housing.

While this list is by no means exhaustive, it provides insight into the myriad of challenges that veterans can face when dealing with PTSD. Each individual's experience is unique, but understanding these common issues can help us empathize with veterans and support them more effectively. We hope this chapter arms you with knowledge and understanding, for it is the first step toward building bridges of support and empathy for our veterans.

Stories of Hope and Recovery

In this chapter, we will explore the narratives of three different veterans who, despite their struggle with PTSD, have managed to carve their paths towards recovery. These stories are a testament to the resilience of the human spirit and an example of the light that can emerge from even the darkest of times.

1. The Story of Anna: From Isolation to Connection

Anna served in Afghanistan for three years. When she returned home, she brought back not just memories of war but a constant state of anxiety that she couldn't shake off. She started having nightmares, replaying traumatic events over and over again in her sleep.

In crowded places, Anna felt overwhelming panic. She isolated herself, avoided social gatherings, and even the simple act of grocery shopping became a hurdle.

Recognizing that she was spiraling, Anna decided to seek help. Her journey began with acknowledging that her experiences had left deep mental scars and it was okay to seek support. She approached a local Veterans Affairs center and started therapy. Her therapist used a combination of cognitive-behavioral therapy and mindfulness techniques to help her manage her symptoms.

But the road to recovery wasn't just about therapy; it was about connection. Anna joined a local support group for veterans where she could share her experiences and hear others' stories. For the first time in a long while, she didn't feel alone. Her support group became her safe space, a place of understanding and acceptance. Today, Anna is a mental health advocate, guiding other veterans on their recovery journey, and turning her struggle into a beacon of hope for others.

2. The Story of Jake: Harnessing the Power of Art

Jake was a marine who served in Iraq. When he came back, he brought with him an unseen wound, a relentless tide of traumatic memories that haunted him. Jake was hyper-vigilant, always on edge, and struggled with sleep. The world felt like a war zone to him, even in the quiet comfort of his home.

He had always been fond of painting, and his therapist suggested using this passion as a form of therapy. Initially, Jake was skeptical. How could painting help him with the demons that lurked in his mind? But he gave it a shot.

Jake began to paint his feelings, his fears, his memories, and his hopes. Each stroke on the canvas was a step towards expressing what he could not put into words. He found a way to externalize his internal struggle, and with every painting, he felt a weight lift off his chest. His paintings weren't just pieces of art; they were pieces of him, his journey, his recovery.

Today, Jake's paintings are a source of inspiration for many. He conducts art therapy workshops for other veterans, helping them use art as a vehicle for healing, just like it was for him.

3. The Story of Maya: The Role of Service Dogs

Maya served in the army for several years. Upon returning, she realized that the battlefield had followed her home. Maya would often wake up in cold sweat, plagued by nightmares of her time at war. Loud noises startled her, and she often found herself scanning her surroundings for threats. Help came in the form of a four-legged friend, a service dog named Max. Max was trained to help veterans with PTSD. He could sense when Maya was getting anxious and would comfort her, distracting her from her distress. At night, Max helped her sleep better, waking her up if she was having a nightmare. Max became Maya's anchor, providing constant comfort and companionship.

Max gave Maya a sense of safety she had long forgotten. With Max by her side, she could go to places she avoided, meet people she had distanced herself from. Over time, with therapy and Max's support, Maya started regaining control over her life. Today, she advocates for the use of service dogs in PTSD treatment, standing as a testament to their incredible healing power. These stories of Anna, Jake, and Maya are examples of how the journey of recovery can take different forms. It's a testament to their strength, resilience, and the promise that, even in the wake of the storm that is PTSD, it's possible to find peace and healing.

Chapter 14: PTSD in Children and Adolescents

It is a common misperception that only adults experience Post-Traumatic Stress Disorder (PTSD). The reality, however, is that children and adolescents can also be significantly impacted by traumatic events and may develop PTSD. Understanding PTSD in young people is crucial because the trauma they experience can profoundly affect their development and overall well-being.

The world can be a confusing and overwhelming place for a child or adolescent. When a traumatic event occurs, it can shake their sense of security and normalcy, leading to deep emotional and psychological distress. It's not just events like accidents or natural disasters that can lead to trauma; situations like bullying, parental divorce, or the death of a loved one can also be traumatic for a young person.

Children and adolescents with PTSD may struggle with intense fear, anxiety, and sadness. They may have nightmares or flashbacks about the event, or they may avoid anything that reminds them of the trauma. Sometimes, they might show changes in behavior or academic performance. Their relationships with family and friends may also be affected.

The good news is, like adults, children and adolescents can recover from PTSD. With the right support, understanding, and treatment, they can navigate the choppy seas of trauma and sail towards calmer waters. In the upcoming sections, we will discuss the symptoms of PTSD in children and adolescents, how it can be diagnosed, and the various treatment options available. We will also explore the ways parents, caregivers, and teachers can support young people dealing with PTSD. Understanding and addressing PTSD in young people is not just about helping them recover from past trauma. It's about ensuring they have the opportunity to grow into healthy, resilient adults.

Understanding Trauma in Children

When we think about trauma, we often picture an adult grappling with the aftermath of a catastrophic event. But children, too, experience trauma, and the impact can be just as significant, if not more. Understanding how trauma affects children and recognizing its manifestations can play a vital role in providing support and facilitating recovery.

Trauma is an emotional response to an overwhelming event that threatens a child's sense of safety and security. It can stem from a wide array of incidents, from a severe car accident to the death of a loved one, and from living in an abusive household to witnessing violence in their community.

Now, let's consider the story of Alex, a seven-year-old boy, who was in a car accident while on a family trip. The event was sudden and terrifying, and although Alex was physically unharmed, the emotional aftermath was intense. He started having nightmares about the accident and became extremely fearful of getting into a car. His parents noticed a change in his behavior - he became more withdrawn, his grades began to slip, and he seemed constantly on edge.

What Alex was experiencing was a form of post-traumatic stress disorder, a condition often associated with adults, but one that affects children as well. His parents, understanding the severity of his emotional distress, sought professional help to guide Alex through his trauma.

A child's experience of trauma can be confusing and frightening. Unlike adults, children often don't have the emotional vocabulary or understanding to articulate what they're going through. They might not say, "I'm feeling scared," or "I'm having flashbacks." Instead, they might show changes in their behavior, have trouble sleeping, or struggle academically.

Each child's response to trauma can be different. Some children might become withdrawn and quiet, while others might act out. Some might develop physical symptoms like stomachaches or headaches. Still, others might regress to earlier behaviors like bed-wetting or thumb-sucking.

It's also important to recognize that the impact of trauma on a child isn't just immediate. Trauma can have long-term effects on a child's mental and physical health. It can interfere with their development, affect their relationships, and even influence their worldview.

But, amid this challenging landscape, there's hope. Children, by nature, are resilient. They have a remarkable ability to heal and recover, especially when they receive the right support. As adults, our role is to provide that support - to be there for them, to validate their experiences, and to guide them towards recovery.

Understanding trauma in children also involves acknowledging our role as adults in their lives. Parents, teachers, and caregivers can all play a significant role in helping a child navigate the aftermath of trauma. It starts with understanding what trauma is, recognizing its signs, and knowing when to seek professional help.

The road to recovery may not be easy, and at times it may seem daunting. But with understanding, patience, and the right resources, we can help our children navigate through their trauma and come out stronger on the other side. Remember, you are not alone in this journey, and neither is your child. There are numerous resources available, including mental health professionals, support groups, and online communities, ready to provide the necessary guidance and support.

Through the following sections, we will explore in detail how to identify the signs of trauma in children, various coping strategies, and potential treatment methods. Understanding trauma in children is the first step towards creating a safe, supportive environment for them to process their experiences and work towards recovery.

Signs and Symptoms

Recognizing the signs and symptoms of trauma in children is crucial. Like Alex, many children who experience trauma may not be able to express their feelings adequately. Instead, their distress often manifests in ways that can easily be mistaken for misbehavior or simply 'going through a phase.'

It's important to remember that every child is unique, and their responses to trauma can be varied and complex. What may seem like a symptom in one child might be a normal behavior in another. The key is to look for changes in behavior, especially those that appear after a traumatic event.

Let's begin by exploring the common signs and symptoms of trauma in children. Please keep in mind that this is not an exhaustive list, and if you notice these signs in a child, it is important to consult a mental health professional for a thorough evaluation and possible diagnosis.

Emotional and Behavioral Changes:

Mood Swings: Children affected by trauma may display unpredictable mood swings. They may quickly shift from being happy to upset without a clear reason.

Anxiety and Fear: They may develop an intense fear related to the traumatic event. For instance, if a child experienced a car accident, they might become anxious about traveling in cars.

Withdrawal: Some children may retreat from social activities and isolate themselves. They might stop participating in activities they once enjoyed.

Irritability and Anger: Children may seem constantly irritable and have frequent outbursts of anger.

Changes in School Performance: A decline in academic performance could be a sign of trauma. Children may struggle to concentrate or lose interest in schoolwork.

Physical Symptoms:

Changes in Appetite and Sleep: A child may eat more or less than usual, have trouble falling asleep, or experience frequent nightmares.

Physical Complaints: Children might complain about physical ailments, such as headaches or stomachaches, with no apparent medical cause.

Restlessness and Hyperactivity: Children might be constantly on the move and find it hard to relax or sit still.

Regression and Other Behavior Changes:

Regression: Children may regress to behaviors they had outgrown, like thumb-sucking or bed-wetting.

Clinginess: Some children may become overly attached and clingy, fearing separation from their caregivers.

Risk-taking or Reckless Behavior: Especially in older children and adolescents, trauma may result in a sudden increase in risk-taking behaviors.

Sarah, a teenager who witnessed a violent incident in her community. Her parents noticed that she became increasingly irritable, and her school performance started to slip. Sarah also started staying out late and hanging out with a new group of friends who were known for their reckless behavior. Her parents realized these changes might be signs of trauma and decided to seek professional help.

The aftermath of trauma can be overwhelming for children and their caregivers, but recognizing these signs and symptoms is the first step towards healing. If you notice these signs in a child, remember, your understanding, empathy, and support can make a significant difference. It's also crucial to seek professional help. A mental health professional can provide a proper evaluation and guide you towards the right resources and treatment.

In understanding the signs of trauma, you arm yourself with the knowledge to be a pillar of support for the child in need. Let's take an instance of Lucy, a caregiver to her niece, Lily. Lily's behavior began to shift markedly following a major upheaval in her life - the sudden loss of her parents. Lucy was perplexed by Lily's dramatic mood swings, her decline in schoolwork, and her constant complaints of stomachaches. Instead of dismissing these as mere signs of grief, Lucy recognized them as potential symptoms of trauma and sought help from a mental health professional. Through this action, Lucy opened the door to support and healing for Lily.

In these situations, a caring and supportive adult can make a world of difference. It's important to remember that children may not understand their own emotions or the reasons behind their actions. They might be scared, confused, and unsure of how to ask for help. As adults, acknowledging their pain, offering reassurance, and seeking professional help are some of the most crucial steps we can take.

A mental health professional is equipped to conduct a thorough evaluation of the child's symptoms, their duration, and how they're affecting the child's daily life. They might use interviews, questionnaires, or other tools to gather information. It's important to share all the noticeable changes you've observed, as well as any known traumatic events the child has experienced.

Once a diagnosis is made, the professional can guide you towards suitable resources and treatment options. These could range from individual therapy, group sessions, family therapy, or even medication in some cases. The primary goal of any treatment plan is to help the child process their traumatic experience in a safe environment, learn coping strategies, and eventually regain their sense of normalcy and control.

The journey might seem long, and the process could be challenging for both the child and the caregiver. But remember, every step forward, no matter how small, is a step towards healing. In this journey, patience, understanding, and love can make the choppy seas seem a little less daunting.

As we proceed further, we'll talk more about the available treatment options and the role of caregivers in helping a child navigate the path to recovery. We'll also discuss strategies that can help children build resilience and provide them with tools they can use to deal with traumatic experiences. By empowering children and their caregivers with the right information and resources, we can turn their journey of healing into a journey of growth and resilience.

Treatment and Support

Facing the waves of trauma is never an easy task, especially for children. Yet, with the right treatment and support, they can learn to navigate these choppy seas with resilience and hope.

Let's explore the realm of support and treatment available for children who have experienced trauma. Picture a vast sea filled with boats of different shapes and sizes - each representing a unique type of support that helps navigate the waters of healing.

Individual Therapy

The most familiar boat perhaps, is individual therapy - a one-on-one interaction with a mental health professional. This form of therapy often adopts evidence-based treatments like Cognitive Behavioral Therapy (CBT) or Eye Movement Desensitization and Reprocessing (EMDR). CBT helps children understand and manage their thoughts and emotions, while EMDR uses bilateral stimulation (like eye movements) to help the child process traumatic memories.

Imagine Jake, a 12-year-old boy struggling with nightmares after witnessing a car accident. Through CBT, he learns to understand his thoughts and emotions, which eventually leads to him managing his fears and reducing the nightmares.

Group Therapy

Sometimes, a larger boat in the form of group therapy serves as the most effective mode of travel. In a group setting, children engage with others who have undergone similar experiences. Sharing and listening to each other's stories can foster a sense of belonging and understanding, making them feel less alone in their journey.

Take the story of Ana, who joined a group therapy session following a natural disaster. Hearing other children recount their experiences made her realize that she wasn't alone in her fear and confusion, offering her a comforting sense of camaraderie.

Family Therapy

The sturdy ship of family therapy holds a crucial place in this sea. Here, the family is viewed as a single unit, and everyone participates in the therapy sessions. This approach can strengthen family ties and promote a supportive environment for the child, aiding in their recovery.

Take the case of Mia, whose parents' divorce triggered her traumatic stress. By attending family therapy, Mia and her parents learned to communicate better, helping Mia to process her feelings and adjust to the changes in her life.

Play Therapy

For younger children who may not articulate their feelings well, a smaller, more colorful boat in the form of play therapy is available. Through creative activities like drawing, playing with dolls, or storytelling, children can express their emotions and trauma indirectly.

Think of little Noah who stopped talking after his pet passed away. His therapist used play therapy to help Noah express his grief and eventually regain his lively spirit.

Medication

At times, the boat might need a small push from a motor, which could be likened to medication. While it's not the first line of treatment, medication can be used in conjunction with therapy to manage certain symptoms like anxiety or depression.

An integrated approach of these various forms of treatment and support can help children reclaim their lives from trauma's grip. The process may seem long, and it requires immense patience, understanding, and love.

This journey towards healing and growth is not to be traveled alone. Professional guidance, family support, and a strong community network can serve as the beacon of light, guiding these young voyagers towards a safe shore. Remember, it's not about how big the waves are, but how well you learn to sail your boat.

Chapter 15: The Journey of Healing

As we embark on this final chapter, we're met with a sight that brings a sense of calm—the prospect of healing from trauma. This journey is not a race, nor is it a straight path. It resembles a winding river, sometimes calm, sometimes rough, but always moving forward towards the vast ocean of recovery and peace.

Just like a river's course is shaped by the terrain it traverses, the healing journey is influenced by our unique experiences, coping mechanisms, and support systems. While PTSD is undoubtedly a storm that disrupts the stillness of life, it is also a catalyst for personal growth and transformation, opening up new pathways of understanding, resilience, and empathy.

Picture, for a moment, a garden hit by a fierce storm. Post-storm, it may appear damaged and chaotic. Yet, with time, sunlight, and nurturing, it begins to bloom again, often with more vibrancy than before. Similarly, with patience, self-care, and professional guidance, healing and growth can occur post-trauma. The key is to remember that you, like that garden, have an inherent capacity to heal and flourish.

The journey of healing is an odyssey through the realms of self-awareness, acceptance, change, and growth. It's about understanding and honoring your feelings, learning to manage symptoms, navigating relationships, creating safe environments, and building a support network.

No two journeys look the same, much like no two rivers follow the exact same path. Yet, they all share a common trait: resilience—the ability to bounce back stronger and more adaptable. This is the beacon that guides us through the often dark and uncertain waters of trauma and PTSD.

Although the journey of healing may be fraught with obstacles, each step taken is a testament to your courage and determination. It's about acknowledging the waves of grief, fear, and confusion, then learning to surf these waves with a newfound strength. It's about harnessing hope and letting it be the sail that propels your boat forward, no matter how choppy the seas may be.

In this chapter, we'll be your guide, providing you with the necessary tools, strategies, and insights to navigate your healing journey. Though we may not be able to calm the storm for you, we can help you to strengthen your boat and become a more skillful sailor. After all, the goal isn't to forget the storm, but to learn how to dance in the rain.

Stages of Healing

The healing journey from trauma is often represented as a process of passing through different stages. Though these stages might not occur in a linear sequence for everyone, understanding them can provide a roadmap, a sense of direction and hope during challenging times.

Stage One: Safety and Stabilization

This initial stage is about establishing a sense of security in your life. Safety can be physical, such as a secure place to live, and psychological, such as feeling safe from sudden intrusive memories or flashbacks. This stage also involves stabilization, which is about learning strategies to manage symptoms of PTSD.

Imagine you're on a ship in the middle of a tempest. The first step to getting through the storm is to secure the ship, tighten loose objects, and ensure the safety of everyone on board. Similarly, in this stage, you'll learn techniques to ground yourself during times of distress, like deep breathing exercises, meditation, or even engaging in physical activities such as yoga or walking.

In addition to individual coping mechanisms, safety and stabilization also involve establishing a supportive environment. This could include a trusted circle of friends and family or a support group. This network can serve as your safe harbor, a place where you can dock your ship during the stormy nights.

Stage Two: Remembrance and Mourning

Once you've established a sense of safety and learned how to manage your symptoms, you might feel ready to explore your trauma narrative, the story of what happened to you. This stage is marked by remembrance and mourning.

To continue the ship analogy, it's now time to assess the damage from the storm. This can be a painful process, as it involves facing the full impact of the trauma. It might involve recalling traumatic memories, expressing feelings about the trauma, and grieving losses associated with it.

During this stage, it's crucial to have professional guidance. A trained therapist can provide a safe space for you to explore your trauma narrative and offer tools and strategies to manage any distress that arises.

Stage Three: Reconnection and Integration

The final stage is about reconnecting with life and integrating the trauma into your identity. Imagine your ship has weathered the storm and reached calm waters. The trauma no longer defines your life, but it has become a part of your journey that has shaped you.

In this stage, you will begin to rebuild aspects of your life that were disrupted by trauma. You might also develop new perspectives, values, and relationships. The experience of trauma can lead to a deep understanding of the preciousness of life, empathy towards others, and a profound appreciation for resilience.

Remember, while these stages provide a framework, everyone's journey is unique. You may oscillate between stages, or find aspects of different stages happening concurrently. That's okay. Healing is not a race, it's about making progress at your own pace, with kindness and compassion for yourself. In this journey, each small step forward is a victory, a testament to your strength and resilience.

Just as a damaged ship can be repaired and even reinforced to become more robust, you too can rebuild from the wreckage of trauma, emerging stronger, more resilient, and full of a renewed sense of life's possibilities. Through this healing journey, you'll discover that the choppy seas you've dealt with have transformed you into a skilled sailor, capable of navigating even the stormiest waters with grace and resilience.

Long-Term Management of PTSD

Living with post-traumatic stress disorder (PTSD) is akin to journeying through an ever-changing landscape. It calls for patience, resilience, and a commitment to long-term management. While it may seem daunting, this voyage offers the potential for personal growth and transformation, a refining process that reveals the strength within you.

Routine and Structure

A structured routine serves as the compass on this journey, offering guidance and a sense of predictability amidst the fluctuating terrain of PTSD symptoms. Regular eating, sleeping, and exercise schedules form a foundation of stability, giving your body and mind the nourishment and rest they need to manage stress.

Balance is key. As tempting as it might be to fill every hour of the day with activities to distract from painful memories, it's crucial to include periods of relaxation and leisure. These calm moments, whether spent in nature, immersed in a book, or engaged in a hobby, provide a necessary counterbalance, a gentle sway against the stronger currents of life.

Continuous Learning and Growth

Your journey through the landscape of PTSD is also a process of continuous learning. Understanding your triggers, recognizing your symptoms, and finding effective ways to manage them are skills that can be developed and honed over time.

Reading about trauma and PTSD, attending workshops or lectures, or participating in online discussions can deepen your understanding and provide you with new strategies. It's like adding more tools to your survival kit. Just remember, what works for one person may not work for another. It's about finding and refining your own unique set of tools.

Connection and Community

People are social creatures. Connection and community can act as a lifeline, a tether of warmth and understanding that can pull you out of the isolation often associated with PTSD.

Support groups offer a space where you can share your experiences, hear others' stories, and realize you're not alone on this journey. Similarly, spending time with loved ones and sharing your thoughts and feelings with them can strengthen your emotional resilience.

Ongoing Therapeutic Support

While self-care strategies are integral to long-term management of PTSD, the guidance of mental health professionals remains essential. Therapists can provide a supportive space for you to explore your feelings and experiences, and psychiatrists can assess and manage any necessary medication.

Embrace this supportive relationship as an alliance, a partnership with experts who can provide valuable insights, yet also respect your autonomy and individual journey. It's like having experienced guides who know the terrain well but understand that it's your journey.

Embracing Self-Compassion

Lastly, as you navigate the long-term management of PTSD, remember to embrace self-compassion. This journey is not about "fixing" yourself or erasing the impact of your trauma. It's about learning to live with your experiences, treating yourself with the same kindness and understanding you would offer to a friend.

Imagine standing at the helm of your ship, your hand steady on the wheel. The waters may be unpredictable, and the journey long, but with the right tools, support, and self-compassion, you have the capacity to navigate through even the toughest storms. You are not defined by the storm but by the courage, resilience, and strength you've shown in navigating your journey. This long-term management of PTSD is not merely about surviving; it's about thriving, discovering your resilience, and steering your ship towards the horizon of hope.

Stories of Recovery and Hope

Let's now turn the pages to a few stories of recovery and hope. These are the narratives of individuals who, like many, have experienced the storms of PTSD but have navigated their way towards healing. While the stories are fictional, they reflect real experiences and illustrate the resilience of the human spirit in the face of adversity.

Story 1: Sara's Journey

Sara, a frontline nurse, was on duty the night her city's hospital received the first COVID-19 patients. Over the next several months, Sara witnessed human suffering on a scale she had never imagined. She was deeply affected by the pain and fear she saw every day, the constant strain of the unknown, and the weight of lives lost despite her best efforts.

Eventually, Sara was diagnosed with PTSD. However, she took the diagnosis as an opportunity to learn about her condition, manage her symptoms, and grow from the experience. Sara built a daily routine that included meditation, balanced nutrition, regular exercise, and adequate sleep. She attended therapy sessions and was an active participant in a local support group. Over time, Sara noticed a change. She was better equipped to manage her anxiety, and the flashbacks gradually lessened.

Sara's journey is a testament to the power of knowledge, self-care, and professional help in the face of trauma. Her story offers hope that while trauma changes us, it does not have to define us.

Story 2: Leo's Resilience

Leo, a war veteran, battled PTSD for many years after returning from active service. Nightmares, intrusive thoughts, and hypervigilance were his constant companions, making his transition to civilian life challenging. However, Leo was determined to reclaim his life from PTSD.

Leo sought professional help and engaged in both talk therapy and Eye Movement Desensitization and Reprocessing (EMDR), a psychotherapy treatment specifically designed to alleviate the distress associated with traumatic memories. He also adopted a service dog, who provided companionship and assistance during panic attacks.

Leo's story underscores the power of resilience and the role of therapeutic support in managing PTSD. It highlights how various forms of therapy, coupled with non-traditional aids like service animals, can contribute to successful long-term management of PTSD.

Story 3: Mia's Connection

Mia was a survivor of childhood abuse. For years, she carried the weight of her past, the trauma manifesting as PTSD in her adulthood. Mia struggled with emotional numbness, a symptom of her PTSD that created a barrier between herself and others. Recognizing that her past was affecting her present, Mia reached out for professional help. Her therapist introduced her to the concept of group therapy, and she decided to give it a try. As she listened to others share their experiences and share her own, Mia began to feel less alone. The group became a lifeline, connecting her to people who understood her journey.

Mia's experience shows the strength found in connection. Her story is a beacon of hope, illustrating that even when trauma leaves us feeling isolated, reaching out can lead to healing, connection, and a shared sense of understanding.

These stories show that the journey of healing is a unique path for everyone. There are different methods, techniques, and routes to arrive at the same destination - a life where trauma is a part of the past, not a determinant of the future. They remind us that recovery is not just possible, but likely when we reach out, seek help, and most importantly, never lose hope.

Conclusion: The Voyage Towards Healing

As we draw our journey through this book to a close, let's reflect on the knowledge we've gained and the stories we've shared. PTSD, as we've learned, is not just a condition but a world that millions, including veterans and civilians alike, find themselves navigating. It's a world where the past overshadows the present, where fear and anxiety cloud the way forward. But it's also a world from which one can emerge stronger, more resilient, and profoundly changed.

While we've delved into the complexities of PTSD, let's remember the book's core message: hope and healing are possible. Like our brave veterans Anna, Jake, and Maya, one can face the turbulence of PTSD and find calm after the storm. Their stories are not just tales of survival; they're narratives of victory against a formidable foe, a testament to the power of human resilience. The key to starting the healing process is acceptance. Acceptance doesn't mean resignation; it means understanding that PTSD is a response to trauma, not a character flaw or a sign of weakness. It means recognizing that seeking help is a strength, not a failure.

Throughout the book, we've offered a variety of strategies for managing PTSD symptoms—from cognitive-behavioral techniques and mindfulness to art therapy and the use of service dogs. These tools are not a one-size-fits-all solution but a palette of options. Each person's path to recovery will be as unique as they are, and it's important to find what resonates and works best for you or your loved ones.

We've emphasized the importance of connection and communication, whether it's through support groups, therapy, or simply heart-to-heart conversations with loved ones. Healing doesn't occur in isolation; it thrives on understanding, empathy, and shared experiences. We've also discussed the challenges that veterans face, acknowledging the unique set of hurdles they must overcome. However, remember that veterans are not their trauma. They are brave individuals who have served their nations, who carry within them strength and resilience that is truly commendable.

To those reading this book who are battling PTSD, remember: It's okay to feel overwhelmed. It's okay to feel scared. But know that you are not alone. There's an entire community here to support you, to journey with you, to hold your hand when the road gets tough. You have within you the strength to weather the storm, to calm the choppy seas, to reach the shores of peace.

As we end, remember that this book is just a steppingstone on your journey towards understanding PTSD. We encourage you to keep learning, keep asking questions, and most importantly, keep believing in your ability to overcome.

Let this book be a beacon, a guide that lights your path, but know that the true power of healing lies within you. Like a lighthouse guiding ships through the night, may it steer you through the choppy seas of PTSD and towards the horizon where hope and healing await. The journey may be long, it may be hard, but remember, the calm always comes after the storm. As we turn the final pages, we hope that this book has given you insight, understanding, and most importantly, hope. Hold on to that hope, for it's the compass that will guide you through the darkest times, towards a future where peace isn't just a dream, but a reality.

In this quest for healing, remember, it's the choppy seas we deal with, but the calm seas that await us. We wish you fair winds and following seas on your journey to recovery.

Epilogue

As you reach the final passages of Surviving PTSD, remember that this book isn't the closing chapter, but merely a steppingstone on your journey to recovery. Post-Traumatic Stress Disorder, or PTSD, is a persistent foe, yet it is one that changes as you grow stronger, more resilient, and better equipped to manage its symptoms. This journey isn't about arriving at a specific destination, but about moving forward, one day at a time, armed with courage, strength, and crucially, hope.

In the aftermath of my own traumatic experiences, I explored a myriad of healing practices: therapy, self-help literature, meditation, and physical activities among others. These conventional coping mechanisms offered strength and wisdom, yet surprisingly, the most transformative relief emerged from an unanticipated source.

During my journey through the choppy sea of PTSD, I stumbled upon a groundbreaking technology that served as a beacon of hope in my darkest hours. This innovation not only offered respite but also sparked a deeper understanding of PTSD and its possible treatments. The healing potential of this technology ignited a curiosity that encouraged me to delve into its intricacies and advantages, providing unique insights into the world of mental health recovery.

Eager to share this newfound knowledge, I extend an invitation to fellow survivors of PTSD, and anyone interested in uncovering innovative methods of dealing with trauma. Much like my own experience, you might discover that this technology soothes some of the raw wounds, alleviates some of the anguish, and reintroduces vibrant hues to a world that seems painfully grayscale post-trauma.

This technology isn't a magical cure, but rather a potential aid offering new approaches for management and healing. It has offered me solace, and I am hopeful that it can extend the same to others navigating their path through PTSD.

As you set this book aside and continue your journey, bear in mind that the process of healing from PTSD isn't a straight line, and everyone's path is unique. Also remember that your resilience is a testament to your strength. Despite the trauma, you are still standing, and that is no small achievement.

In closing, I leave you with a promise and a call to action. The promise is that you are not alone in your struggle. You are a part of a community of survivors who comprehend your pain and share in your resilience. The call to action is to reach out, communicate, and build connections. Collectively, we can navigate the rocky terrains of PTSD towards a haven of acceptance, resilience, and ultimately, a renewed sense of purpose and hope.

If you are interested in knowing more about this new technology, feel free to reach out to me at dee.walterspublishing@gmail.com. Sharing and connecting with others who have walked this path has been a great source of strength for me, and I hope it will be for you, too.

Remain strong, for you are much more formidable than you may believe. Carry your resilience and your lessons as a beacon to guide you through the darkest tunnels. And remember that even after the darkest storms, the sun does rise again.

In strength, resilience, and hope,

The Self-Help Hub